German Cookery for the American Home

Hundreds of Authentic Recipes, Including Soups, Main Meals, Sauces and Desserts

By Ella Oswald

PANTIANOS
CLASSICS

Published by Pantianos Classics

ISBN-13: 978-1-78987-462-4

First published in 1910

Contents

Preface

This representative selection of German recipes, translated into English and adapted to the utensils, weights and measures in use in an English kitchen, will, I trust, prove acceptable to many who, having passed some time in Germany, may like to renew their acquaintance with German cookery. Others, who have made England the land of their adoption, may also find this a useful little book to place in the hands of their English cooks, who will thereby be able more easily to prepare many familiar and favourite dishes unknown to this country.

As a rule, only those recipes have been given whose ingredients are as readily obtainable in England as in Germany. Those have been included, however, whose essentially German components, such as Sardellen (for which Anchovies may be substituted). Sauerkraut, Senfgurken, Pumpernickel, etc., can be easily procured at any of the German Delikatessen Handlungen existing in London and most of our larger towns.

It was whilst staying in the house of a hospitable German friend at Frinton-on-Sea, at all seasons one of most refreshing and idyllic of seaside resorts on our East Coast, that the idea of bringing out a German Cookery Book in our language was first suggested to me. I record this fact from a sense of gratitude to a place that has endeared itself to me and to many others by its never-fading charm: facing the sea, the prettiest of little houses, nestling in their gardens; behind, the wide vista of a delightful countryside, and before them the broad greensward, stretching to the edge of the cliff, whose foot is lapped — or lashed, as the elements may decree — by the waves of the German Ocean.

ELLA OSWALD.

Suppen

(*Soups.*)

Krebs-Suppe
(Crayfish Soup.)

Two Quarts of Soup.   *Time of Preparation:* 2 hours.

24 small crayfish.	Parsley and carraway seeds.
3 oz. butter.	1 teaspoonful chopped fennel.
4 oz. flour.	1 teaspoonful chopped onion,
2 quarts stock.	1½ teaspoonsful Meat
Salt to taste.	Extract.
	Yolks of 2 eggs.

Wash the crayfish in cold water and then boil them for 10 minutes in boiling water, with salt, carraway seeds and parsley. When cold, divide them, leaving the claws (out of which the meat is taken) whole, to put into the soup. The shells of the crayfish may be stuffed and also put into the soup, in which case they should be slit up at the side, that the stuffing can be readily taken out at table. The gall, in the head; the intestine, lying along the tail; and the gray threads lying along the side must be removed altogether. Pound the remaining portions of the shells as finely as possible, then fry in the butter for 2 minutes; add the flour and fry again for 3 minutes. Add the stock, 2 tablespoonsful of carrots and turnips chopped finely, a teaspoonful of chopped fennel, a pinch of carraway and half a teaspoonful of chopped onion. Leave all well covered to simmer for half an hour. Then strain through a sieve and stir in the yolks of 2 eggs, unbeaten. The eggs may also be omitted.

If stuffed crayfish shells or vegetables, such as asparagus, cauliflower, green peas or carrots be served in the soup, they should be boiled in the stock first.

Stuffing for crayfish shells

Take 1 oz. of grated roll, soak and then press out the moisture. Mix with ½ oz. butter and an egg and heat in a pan till it becomes of the consistency of dough. When cold, mix with 1 egg, a teaspoonful of chopped parsley, the meat out of the claws and the crayfish "cream."

Meat or fish balls may be served in the soup instead of the stuffed shells. (*See* sections: Suppen-Einlagen and Fische.)

Aal-Suppe
(Eel Soup.)

3 pints stock.	1 soup-plateful soup herbs.
1 soup-plateful green peas.	Several eels.
1 soup-plateful pears.	Fresh herbs.

Boil for an hour in strong stock a soup-plateful each of green peas, of pears (peeled and cut up into quarters), and of soup herbs (carrots, turnips, celery, etc.) cut into small dice. Add several eels skinned, cut into short lengths and first parboiled with fresh herbs in strongly salted water. Boil all together till tender and thicken the soup, if necessary, with a little butter and flour that have been heated together in a saucepan. Serve with Schwammklösschen.

Schellfisch-Suppe
(Haddock Soup.)

Two Quarts of Soup.   *Time of Preparation:* 2 hours

2 lbs. fish.	2 oz. butter.
3 pints water.	1 onion.
1 pint cream or milk.	Carrots and turnips.
1 teaspoonful of Meat Extract.	Pepper and salt.
2 oz. flour.	

Fillet the fish and cut into small pieces, then boil for 5 minutes in the water the vegetables have been previously boiled in. Mix the butter and flour together and heat in a saucepan, continually stirring until a golden brown; pour the strained stock on to it, add the Meat Extract, the cream or milk, which has been brought to the boil, flavour, put in the fish and serve.

Little fish balls may also be added. If so, then ¼ lb. of the fish should be set aside. The fish should be well dried and put twice through the mincing machine. After this, well pounded in the mortar, pepper and salt, ½ oz. of butter, ½ teaspoonful chopped parsley, a pinch of cayenne and an egg being added during the process. Then pass all through a hair sieve and form into little balls which are thrown into the boiling stock.

Wild-Suppe
(Game Soup.)

One Quart of Soup.   *Time of Preparation:* 2 hours.

2 tablespoonsful fried bread, in dice.	1 partridge, some roast hare or venison.
1 quart stock.	
¼ pint red wine.	1 tablespoonful Madeira

2 tablespoonsful soup herbs (carrots, turnips, celery, parsley, etc.).	½ teaspoonful Meat Extract.

Make stock from 3 pints of water, 2 tablespoonsful of finely chopped soup herbs and a partridge, pigeon or what remains over from roast hare or venison. Thicken the stock as described in Asparagus Soup, with an ounce each of butter and flour, well browned, and allow to simmer for half an hour; then strain. Remove the meat from the bones, pound to a paste in a mortar and add to the stock, together with the red wine, Madeira and a little cayenne.

Angesämte Hühner-Suppe
(Soupe à la Reine.)

Two Quarts of Soup.   *Time of Preparation:* 3 hours.

1 fowl.	4 oz. flour.
¼ pint cream.	4 oz. butter.
2 bitter almonds.	Salt to flavour.
18 sweet almonds.	1 teaspoonful Liebig's Meat Extract.
3 quarts water.	

Boil the fowl in the water till quite tender. Mix the flour and butter together until absolutely smooth and heat in a pan until a delicate brown; then stirring continually, add to the water the fowl has been boiled in. Let the stock simmer gently for half an hour, then strain through a sieve, allow to cool, and skim off the fat. Meanwhile, remove the flesh from off the bones of the fowl and, with the exception of the breast, pound it to a fine paste. Blanch and grate the almonds and then warm the cream almost to boiling point. Now stir the meat, almonds, Meat Extract and cream thoroughly together, add with the breast meat, cut into dice, to the stock and boil up.

Wein-Sappe
(Wine Soup.)

For 6 Persons.   *Time of Preparation:* 1 hour.

1 quart red wine, *or* Moselle, *or* cider, *or* Weissbier.	2 oz. potato flour.
1½ pint water.	A little lemon peel.
	Sugar to taste.

Boil the lemon peel in the water, mix the potato flour well in a quarter of the wine and add to the boiling water. When latter has boiled up again, add the remaining wine and sugar to taste and bring to the boil once more.

If red wine be taken, put ratifia biscuits in, on serving, or place little heaps of whipped white of egg floating on the surface.

If red wine be *not* taken, then the yolks of 2 eggs may be stirred in at the last minute.

Bier-Suppe
(Beer Soup.)

For 6 Persons.   *Time of Preparation:* 1 hour.

1 heaped teaspoonful potato flour.	1 quart water.
1 yolk of egg.	Sugar and salt to taste.
1 quart beer.	

Boil up the beer and water with sugar and salt to taste. Mix the yolk with a teaspoonful of potato flour that has first been mixed smoothly in a little cold water, add gradually some of the boiling beer, stirring continuously, and then pour into the saucepan in which is the rest of the beer. Boil up again and then remove from the fire at once. Stir a little longer and serve.

The white of an egg whisked stiffly with sugar may be put in little heaps on the soup when in the tureen, sprinkled with cinnamon and sugar also, if preferred.

Braunbier-Suppe mit Milch
(Brown Beer Soup with Milk.)

For 6 Persons.   *Time of Preparation:* ½ hour.

1 quart beer (Münchener).	1 tablespoonful rum.
1 pint milk.	2 yolks of eggs.
1 oz. flour.	A stick of cinnamon.
½ oz. butter.	Sugar to taste.

Boil the milk and thicken with half the quantity of flour. Boil the beer separately with a stick of cinnamon, thicken with the rest of the flour, stir in the yolks of eggs, add the boiled milk, and sugar to taste, and stir rapidly for 5 minutes, not immediately over the fire, adding the rum just before serving.

Kartoffel-Suppe
(Potato Soup.)

For 6 Persons.   *Time of Preparation:* 1 hour.

2 quarts water.	4 oz. butter or dripping.
2 lbs. potatoes.	1 oz. flour.
2 sticks celery.	Dried herbs.
1 onion.	A teaspoonful chopped parsley.
A pinch of allspice.	½ teaspoonful Bovril.
A few ground peppercorns.	

Make the butter or fat very hot in a saucepan and then throw in the vegetables, chopped finely, the spice and pepper mixed with an oz. flour, and the, rubbed dried herbs. Then add the water, stirring in a little Bovril and boil until the vegetables are quite soft.

Pass through a sieve and add the chopped parsley.

Fried bread cut in dice may be served with the soup.

Spargel-Suppe
(Asparagus Soup.)

One Quart of Soup.   *Time of Preparation*: 1 hour.

½ lb. asparagus.	1 oz. butter.
1 quart water *or* 1 „ „ in which asparagus has been boiled.	1 oz. flour.
	½ teaspoonful Bovril.
Yolk of 1 egg.	Salt to taste.

Boil the asparagus in the water for 5 minutes. Then take out, cut into small pieces and put back again till tender, when strain off.

Mix the flour and butter together until absolutely smooth and heat in a saucepan, stirring continually until of a golden colour; then, still stirring, add the asparagus water and allow to simmer for half an hour. Strain through a hair sieve, add the Bovril, a lump of butter about the size of a walnut and the pieces of asparagus. Just before serving, stir in the yolk of an egg.

Blumenkohl-Suppe
(Cauliflower Soup.)

This is prepared in the same manner as Asparagus Soup, half a medium-sized cauliflower being taken.

Süddeutsche Zwiebel-Suppe
(South German Onion Soup.)

For 4 Persons.   *Time of Preparation:* 1 hour.

3 onions.	1 tablespoonful flour.
2 yolks.	3 pints stock.
3 oz. butter.	

Cut the onions into small dice and fry a pale golden colour in 3 oz. butter. Stir in a tablespoonful flour and when that is also a pale brown, pour in the stock, stirring well, and boil briskly. Rub through a sieve, boil up again, and finally stir in 2 yolks just before serving.

Sehwerinen-Suppe
(Schwerin Soup.)

1 cucumber, sliced.
Several lettuce hearts.
A few shallots.
1 soup-plateful green peas.
2 - 3 yolks.
Salt and pepper.

1 teaspoonful chopped parsley.
A pinch ground ginger.
3 pints stock.
2 oz. flour.
6 oz. butter.

Cut the cucumber into slices and stew till partly soft in 4 oz. butter with several lettuce hearts, a few young shallots and a plate of green peas. Add the chopped parsley and salt, pepper and a pinch of ground ginger, and then the boiling stock, and boil the soup for an hour. Thicken by stirring in 2 oz. butter, heated with 2 oz. flour, and just before serving, stir in a few yolks of eggs.

Kopfsalat-Suppe
(Thick Lettuce Soup.)

For 6 Persons.   *Time of Preparation:* 1½ hour.

2 oz. butter.
2 sliced onions.
Little bunch of thyme, parsley, chervil.
Juice of half a lemon.
A bayleaf.

2 lbs. of well-washed, dried and shredded lettuces.
3 pints of milk or white stock.
2 oz. ground rice or cornflour.
3 yolks of eggs.
Salt and pepper to taste.

Melt the butter in a saucepan and add the onions, herbs and the lettuces. Simmer for 15 minutes with the lid on.

Next add 3 pints of milk or white stock and 2 oz. of ground rice or cornflour mixed with a little milk. Simmer three-quarters of an hour, skimming well. Rub through a wire or a hair sieve. Put back to get hot and add 3 raw yolks of eggs to each quart of the mixture, the juice of half a lemon, salt, pepper and, if too thick, a little milk. Let the soup thicken, but not boil.

This may be served with a neatly-trimmed poached egg on the top of each helping and a few croutons of fried bread.

Grime Bohnen-Suppe
(Bean Soup.)

One Quart of Soup.   *Time of Preparation:* 1½ hour.

½ lb. French beans.

1½ oz. butter.

¼ pint cream.	1 oz. flour.
1 quart water.	A little nutmeg.
Salt to taste.	½ teaspoonful Bovril.

Cut the beans up finely, pour boiling water over them, then boil in a quart of water. When quite tender, strain. Thicken the water with an oz. of butter and flour, as described in Asparagus Soup, and allow to simmer for half an hour. Then strain, add ½ oz. of butter, ½ teaspoonful of Bovril, ¼ pint of cream, brought almost to the boil, the beans, a little grated nutmeg, bring all just to the boil, and serve.

Erbsen-Suppe
(Pea Soup.)

For 6 Persons.   *Time of Preparation:* 3 hours.

¾ lb. dried peas.	2 quarts stock.
Carrots, turnips.	An onion.

Soak the peas overnight. Then put them on in cold water with a pinch of carbonate of soda and bring to the boil. Strain off the water and pour the stock (preferably prepared from ham) on to the peas, which with the soup herbs must be boiled until quite soft. Then pass all through a sieve, and add a little dried mint or marjoram. Serve with fried bread.

Should green peas instead of the dried ones be taken, which is much to be recommended, then boil separately 1 lb. of carrots, cut into dice and add to the soup on serving, with a teaspoonful of chopped parsley.

Schoten-Suppe
(Green Pea Soup.)

For 6 Persons.   *Time of Preparation:* 2½ hours.

1¼ lb. shelled peas.	¾ oz. frying fat.
2 quarts water.	1 tablespoonful chopped parsley.
½ oz. flour.	½ teaspoonful Bovril.
1½ oz. butter.	

Boil the peas till soft and pass through a sieve.

Brown the flour in the fat and add it with the sugar and a small quantity of Bovril to the stock.

Boil for 10 minutes and then add the chopped parsley and a small lump of fresh butter.

Grünkern-Suppe
(Green Corn Soup.)

For 6 Persons.   *Time of Preparation:* 3 hours.

1 lb. green corn.
¼ pint cream.
2 quarts water.

1 teaspoonful Bovril.
2 eggs.
2 oz. butter.

Wash the green corn well and boil it for 2 hours in the water. Pass through a sieve and stir in the eggs, butter and cream.

Bote Rüben-Suppe
(Beetroot Soup.)

For 6 Persons.   *Time of Preparation:* 3 hours.

3 pints stock.
Half a good-sized beetroot.
1 pint sour cream.
1 oz. flour.

Soup herbs (carrots, turnips, celery, parsley root).
Vinegar, sugar and salt to taste.

Make 3 pints of stock — pork bones may be used for this purpose — putting on a good quantity of soup herbs with the bones. When the stock has been boiling about 2 hours, add a small beetroot, or half a large one, peeled and chopped small, and boil for another half-hour. Then strain and add salt to taste, and a little vinegar in which sliced beetroot has been standing. If no beetroot vinegar is to hand, then grate a piece of beetroot, mix it with the juice of a lemon and add instead of the vinegar. Finally, mix the flour and cream smoothly, and add with a trifle sugar and Bovril to the soup, which should be allowed just to come to the boil.

Sellerie-Suppe
(Celery Soup.)

For 6 Persons.   *Time of Preparation:* 2 hours.

1 large celery root.
1 pint water.
3 pints thickened stock.

1 oz. butter.
½ teaspoonful Bovril.

Peel the celery, cut it into rounds, and boil it until quite soft. Strain the water off, add to it the butter and then the thickened stock (made from 2 quarts of water, 1 oz. butter, 1 oz. flour, as described in Asparagus Soup). Pass through a sieve, flavour with Bovril, and serve.

Birnen-Suppe
(Pear Soup.)

For 6 Persons.   *Time of Preparation:* 1½ hour.

2 lbs. pears.	Sugar to taste.
1 quart water.	A stick of cinnamon.
1 gill sweet or sour cream.	1 oz. flour.
½ teaspoonful aniseed.	

Wash and peel the pears and set them on to boil with the aniseed, cinnamon stick and peelings. When they have boiled 5 minutes, strain off the water, and cut up the pears into small pieces. Put back into the water and boil until quite soft.

Beat the flour and cream to a smooth paste, add to the pears and flavour with sugar and salt to taste.

Semolina dumplings (see recipe, page 17) are a good addition to this soup.

Fruit syrup or wine may be substituted for the cream; in this case omit the aniseed.

Apfel-Suppe
(Apple Soup.)

For 6 Persons.   *Time of Preparation:* 1 hour.

2 lbs. apples.	1 oz. potato flour.
2½ pints water.	Sugar to taste.

Wash the apples, cut them up into small pieces, boil till soft in the water, with some cinnamon, and then pass through a sieve. Thicken with potato flour and add sugar to taste. Bread cut into dice and fried in butter, or ratifias are served with the soup. This soup may be varied by boiling a little rice, sago, or semolina in the water first and then adding the apples, peeled and cut up small.

Kirsch-Suppe
(Cherry Soup.)

1 lb. cherries.	½ oz. potato flour.
2½ pints water.	Sugar to taste.

Put on the cherries in the water, boil a quarter of an hour, pass through a sieve, thicken the soup with potato flour and serve with fried bread or little dumplings. (See section: Suppen-Einlagen, Klösse.)

14

Pflaumen-Suppe
(Plum Soup.)

1½ lb. plums.
2½ pints water.

1½ oz. potato flour.
Sugar to taste.

Prepare as for Cherry Soup.

Blaubeer-Suppe
(Bilberry Soup.)

1½ lb. bilberries,
2½ pints water.

1½ oz. potato flour.
Sugar to taste.

Prepare as for Cherry Soup.

Johannisbeer-Suppe
(Currant Soup.)

1 lb. of currants.
2½ pints of water.

1½ oz. potato flour.
Sugar to taste.

Prepare as for Cherry Soup.

Preisselbeer-Suppe
(Cranberry Soup.)

1 lb. cranberries.
1½ oz. potato flour.

2½ pints water.
Sugar to taste.

Prepare as for Cherry Soup.

Holunder-Suppe
(Elderberry Soup.)

½ lb. elderberries.
½ lb. plums.
2 oz. potato flour.

Sugar to taste.
3 pints water.

Prepare as for Cherry Soup.

Hagebutten-Suppe
(Rose-Hip Soup.)

For 6 Persons.   *Time of Preparation:* 1 hour.

½ lb. dried rose hips.   2 oz. potato flour.
3 pints water.   Sugar to taste.

Wash the hips, soak them some hours in water and then let them simmer till quite soft, when pass through a sieve. Boil up again, adding sugar, thicken with potato flour and serve, either with or without Nudeln, Einlauf or little dumplings. (For recipes for latter, see section: Suppen-Einlagen, Klösse.)

Backpflaumen-Suppe
(Prune Soup.)

Prepare in the same manner as Rose-Hip Soup.

Milch-Suppe
(Milk Soup.)

One Quart of Soup.   *Time of Preparation:* 1 hour

1 quart milk.   Salt.
1 egg.   A little flour

Thoroughly mix the egg with enough flour to make a smooth, stiff paste, which will drop irregularly off the spoon. Put the milk on to boil, and when boiling, drop this paste slowly into it, and salt to taste. Sugar and cinnamon may be used instead of salt to flavour the soup.

Milch-Suppe mit Mandeln
(Milk Soup with Almonds.)

One Quart of Soup.   *Time of Preparation:* ½ hour.

1 quart milk.   1 teaspoonful grated bitter almonds.
1 oz. potato flour.   2 oz. grated sweet almonds.
1 oz. sugar.   A pinch of salt

Put the milk on to boil with the almonds, sugar and a pinch of salt, reserving a small quantity of the milk to mix cold with the potato flour to a smooth paste. When the milk boils, stir in the dissolved potato flour and boil a few minutes longer.

This soup may be served hot or cold.

Schokoladen-Suppe
(Chocolate Soup.)

3 pints milk.
1 teaspoonful potato flour.
4 oz. chocolate.

2 yolks of eggs.
Sugar and salt to taste.
2 whites of eggs.

Put the milk on to boil with the chocolate grated finely, reserving a small quantity to mix cold with the potato flour. When the milk boils, stir in the dissolved potato flour and then the yolks of 2 eggs. Sweeten with sugar to taste. Whisk the whites of eggs to a stiff snow, and place in rough heaps on the soup when in the tureen. This soup may be served hot or cold.

Brod-Suppe
(Bread Soup.)

1 quart water.
4 oz. German bread.

1 oz. butter.
Salt.

I.

Cut the bread into small pieces, pour the water over it, let it stand for an hour, then bring it to the boil, pass through a sieve, add the butter and salt to taste, and bring once more to the boil.

II.

With the soup prepared as described, 1 lb. of apples may be boiled and passed through the sieve with the bread. Add sugar and lemon peel to taste. Prunes may be substituted for the apples.

III.

Soup No. I. may also be varied by the addition of a little Meat Extract.

Wein-Kaltschale
(Cold Wine Soup.)

1 pint white wine.
1 pint water.
A sliced lemon.

A few pieces cinnamon.
Sugar to taste.

An hour before serving, place in a tureen Suppenmakronen or ratifia biscuits and pour over them equal quantities of wine and water, adding a few pieces of cinnamon, some slices of lemon (without pips) and sugar to taste. Stand on ice, if possible, until required.

Bier-Kaltsohale
(Cold Beer Soup.)

1 quart beer (Weissbier *or* Lager).
1 tablespoonful grated German bread.
A little lemon peel.

1 pod of cardamom, pounded.
¼ pint water.
A slice of lemon.
2 oz. currants, boiled in water.

Mix all ingredients well and stand in a cool place, on ice if possible. Serve with ratifias, or Suppenmakronen.

Suppen-Einlagen. Klösse

(Dumplings, etc., served with Soup, Meat, or Fruit.)

Reis zar Suppe.
(Rice.)

For 6 Persons.   *Time of Preparation:* 1¼ hour.

4 oz. rice.
1 oz. butter.

1 pint strong stock.
1 oz. Parmesan cheese.

Scald the rice and put it on with the stock and butter to simmer for an hour till quite soft. Then stir in the cheese. Rinse a shape with cold water, press the rice into it and leave it for 5 minutes. Then turn it out on to a dish, sprinkle chopped parsley over it and hand round with the soup.

It will be found an improvement to stir in 2 eggs, beaten up in a tablespoonful of water, just as the rice is soft; it must then be brought up to the boil again.

Grieswürfel
(Semolina Dice.)

For 6 Persons.   *Time of Preparation:* 1¼ hour.

1 pint stock.   1 oz. butter.   4 oz. semolina.

Throw the semolina into the boiling stock and stir continually until the whole becomes stiff. Then spread on a dish to the thickness of about 1/3-inch and allow to cool. When quite cold, cut up into little dice and add to the soup on serving.

Griesklösschen
(Semolina Dumplings.)

For 8 Persons.   *Time of Preparation:* 1 hour.

½ pint milk.	3 eggs.
2 oz. butter.	Pinch of grated nutmeg *or* 4 bitter
Salt.	almonds.
4 oz. semolina.	

Boil up the milk with the butter in it, then stirring continually, strew in the semolina and continue stirring until the whole becomes a solid mass. Now remove from the fire and stir in 1 egg, salt and a pinch of grated nutmeg (or 4 grated bitter almonds). When cool, stir in the other eggs.

Form into little balls and boil for 3 minutes in the soup.

Einlanf

For 6 Persons.   *Time of Preparation:* 10 minutes.

3 oz. flour.	1 tablespoonful water.
2 eggs.	Pinch of grated nutmeg.

Beat all ingredients well together to a stiff, smooth paste, and drop slowly from the end of a spoon, or through a colander, into the boiling soup, shortly before serving.

Einlauf von geriebener Semmel
(Einlauf of Grated Roll.)

For 6 Persons.   *Time of Preparation:* 10 minutes.

3 eggs.	1 teaspoonful chopped parsley.
4 oz. grated roll.	

Stir all ingredients well together and press through a colander into the boiling soup, shortly before serving.

Eierstich

¼ pint stock.	3 eggs.
½ teaspoonful salt.	Pinch of nutmeg.

Beat all the ingredients well together and put into a well-buttered shape, or into several little shapes, which place into very hot (but not boiling) water, till the paste is of the firmness of bacon. Then if a large shape has been used, cut up into dice, and serve in the soup. The small shapes are turned out whole into the soup.

Wiener Nockerl

For 6 Persons.   *Time of Preparation:* 1 hour.

2 oz. butter.   Yolks of 2 eggs.
3 oz. flour.   White of 1 egg.
Pinch of white pepper.   ½ teaspoonful salt.

Cream the butter, add the eggs and salt and finally the flour, and stir for 10 minutes. Then spread a quarter of an inch thick on a moist pasteboard, cut into dice, or other small shapes, and boil for a minute in the soup before serving.

Nudeln

For 6 Persons.   *Time of Preparation:* ¾ hour.

4 oz. flour.   ½ teaspoonful salt.
The yolk of 1 egg.   A pinch of grated nutmeg.

Mix the flour with the salt and nutmeg. Make a hole in the middle, put in the beaten yolk of egg, mix into the flour and knead the dough well. It must be very stiff.

Roll out very thinly and cut into strips. Place these strips over a cloth on the back of a chair to dry. Then cut them into narrower strips of about ½-inch wide and 2 inches long.

Throw these into salted boiling water and boil for 20 minutes. If required for soup, Nudeln may either be boiled first and then put into the stock, or thrown straight into the boiling soup.

Another way of treating Nudeln is to drain them, when sufficiently cooked, and put them on a hot dish, serving with brown butter or tomato sauce, or use them in place of macaroni, in macaroni cheese. The nutmeg may be omitted, if preferred.

Spritzklösse

½ gill water.   2 eggs.
3 oz. flour.   1 oz. Parmesan cheese.
1 oz. butter.

Mix the flour and water perfectly smoothly, add to the butter, which has previously been melted, and stir continually, till the whole becomes a solid mass. Then stir in the cheese and eggs till a smooth paste is obtained. Roll a piece of paper to the shape of a funnel, put the paste into it and sprinkle into the boiling soup.

Suppenmakronen
(Soup Macaroons.)

Whites of 3 eggs.
4 oz. castor sugar.
2 oz. sweet almonds.

6 bitter almonds,
5 oz. grated roll.

Whisk the whites of eggs with the sugar, then add the grated roll and almonds (previously mixed together) and stir to a smooth paste. With a teaspoon place in little heaps on a well-buttered tin and bake a golden brown.
A nice addition to Wine, Beer, Fruit, and Milk Soups.

Schwammklösse

Whites of 2 eggs
A little milk
A breakfastcupful flour.

Butter, the size of 2 walnuts
2 yolks.
A little ground mace.

Put 2 whites of eggs in a breakfastcup, fill it up with milk and put into a saucepan with a breakfastcupful of flour and a lump of butter equal in size to 2 walnuts. Stir well over the fire till the paste becomes so thick that it comes away from the sides of the saucepan and forms a ball. Remove from the fire and, when cool, stir in 2 beaten-up yolks of eggs and a little ground mace. Cut out little balls of this paste with a spoon, throw into the boiling soup, and boil till they rise to the surface

Kalbfleischklösse
(Veal Balls.)

For 6 Persons.   *Time of Preparation:* ½ hour.

2 tablespoonsful cream.
½ lb. veal.
3 oz. bacon.
3 oz. grated roll.

A pinch of salt.
A pinch of pepper.
1 teaspoonful chopped parsley.
2 eggs.

Pass the meat and bacon twice through the mincing machine. Stir the grated roll into the cream, add the eggs, salt, pepper, parsley, and lastly the meat.
Form into balls the size of a hazelnut and boil them for 5 minutes in the soup.

Rindfleischklösse
(Beef balls.)

For 6 Persons.   *Time of Preparation:* 1 hour.

½ lb. beef.   Pinch of salt.
1 oz. breadcrumbs.   Pinch of pepper.
2 oz. butter.

Pass the meat twice through the mincing machine. Cream the butter, and add to it the egg, breadcrumbs, salt, pepper, and lastly the meat, mixing thoroughly. Form into little balls and boil for 5 minutes in the soup.

Leberklösse
(Liver Balls.)

For 6 Persons.   *Time of Preparation:* 1 hour.

6 oz. calves' or fowls' liver.   2 oz. flour.
1 oz. bread, cut into small dice and Salt and pepper to flavour.
fried in 1 oz. butter.   1 teaspoonful chopped parsley.
2 eggs.   1 oz. butter.

Pass the liver through the mincing machine. Then stir into it the salt, parsley, pepper, egg, flour, the butter (previously melted), and lastly the bread, fried. Form into little balls and boil for 4 minutes in the soup.

Markklösschen
(Marrow Balls.)

3 oz. beef marrow.   ½ tablespoonful chopped parsley.
2 eggs.   Pinch of salt.
4 oz. grated roll.

Melt the marrow in a saucepan, beat to a froth, add the 2 eggs, stir in the grated roll and salt, mix well and form into little balls. Boil for 3 minutes in the soup.

Mehlklösse mit gerösteter Semmel

For 6 Persons.   *Time of Preparation:* ¾ hour.

2 oz. roll, cut into dice and fried in   2 whole eggs.
butter.   1 pint milk.
Salt.   10 oz. flour.

Make the well-beaten eggs, milk and flour into a paste, mixing well. Stir in the fried bread or roll. Cut off small pieces with a spoon, throw them into boiling water and boil for 5 minutes.

Pour browned butter over them and serve with stewed fruit or meat.

Feine Mehlklösse

For 6 Persons.　　　　　*Time of Preparation:* 1 hour.

1 lb. flour,	1 tablespoonful sugar.
1 ½ oz. butter,	1 tablespoonful grated roll.
¾ pint milk.	A little lemon juice *or*
4 eggs.	4 bitter almonds.
Salt.	

Melt the butter in a saucepan, add to it the milk thickened with flour and salt, and heat, stirring well, until of the consistency of dough. Then remove from the fire and, when cool, stir in gradually the beaten-up eggs, grated roll, sugar and grated almonds or lemon peel. Cut off small pieces with a table-spoon, throw into boiling water and boil 4 minutes.

Semmelklösse

6 oz. roll,	4 bitter almonds, grated.
½ lb. flour.	1 tablespoonful salt.
¾ pint milk.	2 eggs.
2 oz. butter.	

Cut the roll into small dice, pour milk over them and stir well. Then add the well-beaten eggs, the butter, melted, salt and grated almonds and mix well. Cut off small pieces of this paste with a tablespoon, throw into boiling water and boil, with the lid on, for 5 minutes.

Kartoffelklösse
(Potato Dumplings.)

For 6 Persons.　　　　　*Time of Preparation:* 1 hours.

2 lbs. potatoes.	2 tablespoonsful grated roll.
1 oz. butter.	A pinch of pepper or nutmeg.
1 egg.	3 oz. flour.
1 tablespoonful salt.	

Boil the potatoes and rub them through a sieve when cold. Stir into them a beaten-up egg, a tablespoonful salt, pepper, the butter melted, the flour and grated roll and mix thoroughly to a paste. Form into little balls, roll in flour, throw into boiling water and boil with the lid on for 6 minutes.

If these dumplings are to be served with fruit, add a little sugar, 4 grated bitter almonds and another egg in making the paste, and omit the.pepper.

Apfelklösse
(Apple Dumplings.)

For 6 Persons. *Time of Preparation:* 2 hours.

1 lb. apples.	14 oz. flour.
3 eggs.	1 oz. butter.
1 gill milk.	1 teaspoonful salt.

Peel and core the apples and cut them into little dice. Mix the remaining ingredients to a firm paste and stir the apples into it. Cut off small pieces with a tablespoon, throw into boiling water and boil a few minutes. Serve with brown butter, sprinkled over with sugar and cinnamon.

Klösse von rohen Kartoffeln
(Dumplings made from Raw Potatoes.)

For 6 Persons. *Time of Preparation:* 2 hours.

3 lbs. peeled raw potatoes.	1½ oz. roll cut into small dice.
3 oz. semolina.	¾ pint milk.
2 oz. butter.	1 tablespoonful salt.

Grate the potatoes under water, to preserve a good colour, then pour into a jelly bag and press all the water out. Cut the roll into small dice and fry in butter. Boil the semolina in the milk to a purée and pour it, while boiling, over the potatoes. Add salt and stir in the roll, mixing thoroughly.

Form into 12 little balls, throw into boiling water, salted, and boil for 20 minutes.

Serve with Sauerkohl, roast meat, etc.

Württembergischer Hützelkloss

For 6 Persons. *Time of Preparation:* 3½ hours.

1 lb. flour.	3 oz. sugar.
1 oz. breadcrumbs soaked in milk.	¾ lb. stewed prunes and other dried
The grated rind of ½ lemon.	fruits; pears, apple-rings, apricots,
2 pounded cloves.	etc. (Backobst).
8 bitter almonds.	½ oz. baking powder.

| ½ lb. suet. | 1 tablespoonful salt. |
| 3 eggs. | |

Chop the suet finely and mix it with the flour. Press the milk partly out of the breadcrumbs and stir them smoothly with the eggs, grated lemon peel, almonds, ground cloves and the salt and baking powder. Then add the flour gradually and knead to a dumpling. Place on a plate that will stand in a saucepan and pour sufficient boiling water on to three parts cover the dumpling. Cover the saucepan and boil 15 minutes. Then arrange on the plate, round it, the stewed Backobst (previously soaked an hour or two) mixed with sugar. Simmer gently for another 2 hours.

Serve with cold boiled ham.

Tiroler Klösse
(Tyrolean Dumplings.)

For 6 Persons.	*Time of Preparation:* 30 minutes.

½ lb. boiled chopped ham.	2 oz. flour.
1 oz. butter.	1 tablespoonful chopped parsley.
2 eggs.	5 oz. breadcrumbs.

Cream the butter, stir into it the beaten-up eggs, then the breadcrumbs, chopped ham, flour and parsley, and mix well. Form into little dumplings and boil 8 minutes in slightly salted water. Pour browned butter over and serve, sprinkled with Parmesan cheese.

Tomato sauce is an excellent addition. In the Tyrol these dumplings are boiled in beef stock and served with it.

Gobackene Klösse zn Obst
(Fried Dumplings with Fruit.)

2 lbs. flour.	1 breakfastcupful oiled butter.
3 eggs.	1 oz. yeast.
¾ pint milk.	2 tablespoonsful sugar.

Stir in half the flour with the milk, salt, eggs and yeast, and allow to rise. When risen, stir in the remaining flour, butter and sugar, and knead the dough well. Cover and stand in a warm place to rise again slowly. Form into little balls by rolling out very thickly and cutting out with a wineglass. Let these rise a third time and throw into a saucepanful of frying butter for 10 minutes.

Dampfnudeln

Prepare the dough as in preceding recipe. When the dumplings have risen a third time, put them in a deep pan in which plenty of butter has been browned slightly. Pour in ½ pint milk, cover tightly and place a damp cloth over, in addition. After 10 minutes, when the under sides of the dumplings are somewhat brown, turn them and let them get brown on the other side, the saucepan now remaining uncovered.

The dumplings can also be boiled for ½ hour in salted water.

Serve with brown butter and fruit

Fische
(*Fish.*)

Fische im Wasserbade gekocht
(Steamed Fish.)

This method of preparing fish is the most delicate, as well as the most wholesome.

For 6 Persons.   *Time of Preparation:* 1 hour.

2 lbs. fish.	1 onion.
1½ to 2 tablespoonsful salt.	1 parsley root.
1 piece celery.	A few peppercorns.

Clean the fish thoroughly, rub the salt well into it, place it in an enamel stewpan, or small enamelled fish-kettle, with the onion, celery, and parsley-root (all cut up) and peppercorns arranged round it, and stand the pan, covered, in a cool place for half an hour.

Then place the stewpan, still firmly closed, in a larger saucepan or fish-kettle, in which there is sufficient boiling water to come to the top of the contents in the inner pan. Cover this outer saucepan tightly so that no steam may escape and keep the water boiling for 25 to 30 minutes. To ascertain whether the fish is sufficiently boiled, the lids must of course be lifted from each saucepan, and when the steam has been allowed to escape, the condition of the fish can be tested with a larding needle. If the meat lifts readily off the backbone, then the fish is done.

Serve with butter, melted or browned, or with various sauces (*see* recipes under section "Sauces"), for the making of which the broth that has formed during the cooking of the fish should be used.

Salmon should not be prepared in this manner, but haddock and cod are excellent so prepared.

Fisch mit pikanter Sauce
(Fish with Piquant Sauce.)

For 8 Persons. *Time of Preparation:* 1 hour.

4 lbs. haddock *or*	1 oz. salt.
2½ lbs. pike, perch, carp, etc.	½ teaspoonful Liebig's Meat Extract,
4 oz. butter.	dissolved in 1/3 pint water.
½ oz. flour.	½ tablespoonful chopped parsley.
A few bottled mushrooms.	2 tablespoonsful chopped onion.
A pinch of cayenne.	1 tablespoonful capers.
½ teaspoonful English mustard,	2 tablespoonsful lemon juice

Clean the fish well, cut it into medium-sized pieces, rub them over with salt and parsley, and stand in a cool place for 10 minutes.

Mix the butter, flour, mustard, and cayenne to a stiff paste. Cover the bottom of a stewpan with small lumps of this paste, add half the quantity of the onions, capers, and mushrooms. Put in the pieces of fish, and then the rest of the paste in small pieces, and the remainder of the onions, capers, and mushrooms. Pour over this the lemon juice and the water in which the Meat Extract should first have been dissolved.

Cover the stewpan tightly and stand it in a larger saucepan, in which there is sufficient boiling water to come to the level on the top of the contents in the inner pan. Cover this outer saucepan tightly, to prevent any steam escaping, and keep the water boiling 20 to 25 minutes. Then take out the inner stewpan, bring the fish just to the boil and serve.

Fisch mit Tomaten
(Fish with Tomatoes.)

For 8 Persons. *Time of Preparation:* 1½ hour.

4½ lbs. fish (haddock, cod, gurnet, etc.).	A pinch of pepper.
	½ teaspoonful Liebig's Meat
1 oz. salt.	Extract, dissolved in 3 tablespoonsful
6 oz. butter.	water.
½ oz. flour.	1 tablespoonful chopped parsley.
2 oz. chopped onion.	2 tablespoonsful tomato purée.

Clean the fish well, dry it thoroughly, cut it up into medium-sized pieces, rub over well with salt and pepper, and stand in a cool place for about lo minutes. Mix the butter, flour, onion, and parsley well together to a stiff paste. Cover the bottom of a stewpan or mould with small lumps of this paste. Pour a third of the tomato purée over them, then put in the pieces of fish and cover with the remainder of the purée.

Pour over this the water with the Meat Extract dissolved in it, cover the stewpan tightly and place it in a larger saucepan in which there is sufficient boiling water to come to the level of the top of the contents in the inner pan. Cover this outer saucepan tightly to prevent any steam escaping, and keep the water boiling for 30 minutes. Then take out the inner stewpan, bring the fish just to the boil and serve.

Schlei in Dillsauce
(Tench with Dill Sauce.)

2½ lbs. tench.	1 onion.
½ oz. butter.	1 tablespoonful chopped parsley.
1 oz. flour.	1 tablespoonful chopped dill.
1 gill cream.	A pinch of pepper.
1 parsley root.	A pinch of salt.

Mix the butter and flour together to a stiff paste. Place little lumps of this paste in a stewpan with the parsley root (cut in two), an onion, and some of the chopped parsley and dill. On this place the fish, which has been well cleaned, cut into medium-sized pieces and rubbed over with salt, and cover the fish with the remainder of the paste, in little lumps, and a little more of the dill and parsley. Pour over this the cream and cover the stewpan tightly.

Place the pan in a larger saucepan, in which there is sufficient boiling water to come to the top of the contents in the inner pan. Cover this outer saucepan tightly, so that no steam may escape, and keep the water boiling for 25 to 30 minutes. Then take out the inner stewpan and put it directly on the fire, so that the fish comes just to the boil. Then add the remainder of the chopped parsley and dill. Before serving, remove the parsley root and the onion

Fische auf einfache Art gekocht
(Fish — Plain boiled.)

Fischblau
(Fish prepared to appear Blue.)

The most suitable fish to be prepared in this manner are: Carp, tench, bream, trout, eel, and salmon.

To prepare a fish so that when boiled it appears bluish, do not scrape off the scales when cleaning, and pour over it dilute hot vinegar, leaving it then exposed to the air for a while. The blue colour is produced by the action of the vinegar and air on the colouring matter of the skin.

After this treatment, put the fish on in cold salt water, allowing about 2 oz. salt to every quart of water, and adding some peppercorns, onions and soup herbs (carrots, parsley root, celery, etc.). It is advisable to boil the onions and soup herbs previously in a little water for half an hour and to add the broth so obtained to the water in which the fish is boiled, as it takes longer to extract the goodness out of the vegetables by boiling than to boil the fish.

Fish boiled whole should be tied to the drainer of the fish-kettle.

Large fish must be brought slowly to the boil, small fish quickly, the lid being kept on the fish-kettle. The fish should then be placed a little on one side and allowed to simmer quite gently till done. Then dash a little cold water over it and let it remain a few minutes longer in the kettle before serving.

To ascertain whether the fish is done, insert a larding needle carefully into the middle of the back. If the flesh is readily lifted from the backbone, then the fish is done. Lift out the drainer with the fish on it, allow the water to strain off thoroughly, remove quickly the thread which has kept the fish in place, and slide the latter on to a dish, which may, or may not, be covered with a serviette. Garnish with parsley and small boiled potatoes.

Serve with brown butter sauce (with or without German mustard), or merely oiled butter, or Dutch, Mushroom, Caviar, or Oyster Sauce. Mayonnaise or Remoulaclen Sauce may also be taken. (*See* section "Sauces" for the various recipes.) Every kind of fish can be boiled in this manner, without being rendered bluish, the fish being merely thoroughly cleaned and the scales removed.

Lachsblan
(Boiled Salmon.)

Clean and wash the salmon, leaving the scales on, however, if the fish is to appear bluish. In this case pour over it a little dilute boiling vinegar, then' let it stand a few minutes and tie it on to the drainer, placing latter into the fish-kettle. Pour over it sufficient cold water, strongly salted (2 oz. to the quart) to cover the fish well. Add plenty of onions, carrots, turnips, parsley root, and celery and half a gill of Tarragon vinegar. Bring slowly to the boil, covered, and then stand on one side to simmer very gently ½ to ¾ hour, according to size of the fish. (*See* last recipe for ascertaining when a fish is sufficiently boiled for serving.) When done, leave in the fish-kettle for another quarter of an hour. Serve on a long dish, garnished with parsley and slices of lemon. Hand round with it oiled butter, Dutch sauce, whipped cream with horseradish, etc. (*See* section "Sauces" for the various recipes.)

Seezunge gekocht
(Boiled Sole.)

Reckon about ½ lb. sole to each Person.   *Time of Preparation: ¾ hour.*

Smaller fish are boiled without being skinned. Larger ones should always be skinned. To do so, cut through the skin very carefully just round the tail and by the fins, and loosen it by slipping a knife under it. Then hold the fish firmly by the tail with a cloth and draw off the skin carefully from the tail towards the head. Both the white and the grey skins must be removed. Clean the fish well, lay it on a fish-slice and put it on to boil in cold water, strongly salted (1 oz. salt to the quart of water) and with a little lemon juice in it. Bring to the boil and then stand on one side to simmer very gently for another 10 minutes. Serve on a hot dish, garnished with parsley. Dutch, Mushroom or Oyster Sauce should be handed round with it. (*See* various recipes in section "Sauces.")

Flonder gekocht
(Boiled Plaice.)

Skin and clean the plaice. Strew salt over it and leave to stand for 2 hours. Then boil in the same manner as sole (*see* previous recipe), adding onions to the water. Serve with Dutch Sauce.

Forellen
(Trout.)

Clean the trout thoroughly, leave the scales on and pour some hot vinegar over them to make them bluish. Then stand on one side for a little while.

Pass a thread of cotton through the head and tail of each fish, tying it together, so that the fish forms a ring.

Fill the fish-kettle with very slightly salted water. When the water is boiling furiously, plunge in the drainer on which the trout have been arranged.

Then immediately remove from the fire again. Small trout are sufficiently cooked by the mere plunging into boiling water — larger ones should be allowed to remain in the water for 3 minutes after the fish-kettle has been removed from the fire.

Serve on a dish covered with a serviette, first removing the threads carefully. Garnish with parsley, crisp lettuce leaves and slices of lemon.

Fresh butter in little balls or rolls, or oiled butter with chopped parsley in it, should be handed round with the trout, which must always be served very hot.

Fische in Sauce gekocht
(*Fish Boiled in Sauce.*)

Fisch in weisser Sauce oder grüner Fisch
(Fish in White Sauce.)

For 8 Persons.	*Time of Preparation:* 2 hours.
3½ lbs. fish.	6 oz. butter.
2½ pints white sauce.	10 sweet almonds, grated

| 2 teaspoonsful chopped parsley. | 1 gill cream. |
| 1 teaspoonful chopped onion. | A pinch of salt and pepper. |

Fish suitable for this method of preparation are: Haddock, pike, perch, fresh herring, plaice, tench and cod.

Fish to be boiled in white sauce must be most thoroughly cleaned or the flavour of the sauce will suffer. Scrape off all the scales, as well as cleaning.

With haddock, cod, herring and plaice remove the head altogether; with the other fish, it may be cooked with it, but should be well scraped. Cut the fish when cleaned into medium pieces, and place (in cases where the heads are retained, the heads should be placed lowermost) in 2½ pints of white sauce (*see* recipe), which should be hot, but not boiling. Bring slowly to the boil, add the butter, chopped onions, grated almonds, pepper and the cream, and finally, when the fish is done, the finely-chopped parsley. Then stand on one side for 25 minutes, not allowing further boiling.

Should fresh herrings be taken for this dish, the white sauce should be quite cold when they are put into it, and should then be brought quickly to the boil.

Seezongenrollen in Champignon-Sauce
(Rolled Soles in Mushroom Sauce.)

For 8 Persons.   *Time of Preparation: 2 hours.*

4½ lbs. soles.	1 tablespoonful lemon juice.
1½ pint white sauce.	½ teaspoonful Liebig's Meat Extract.
1 gill Rhine wine.	A small bottle of mushrooms.
4 oz. butter.	A pinch of salt.
5 yolks of eggs.	

Skin and fillet the soles carefully. Sprinkle salt over each fillet, roll and tie round with a thread. Make ij pint white sauce (see recipe, page 55), salt it very slightly and stir into it half a teaspoonful of Liebig's Meat Extract. Warm up the sauce in an enamel saucepan, place the rolled fillets in it and boil for 3 minutes. Then take out and place on a hot dish. Add to the sauce the mushrooms, cut in two, and the butter. Stir in the yolks of eggs, flavour with lemon juice, pour over the soles and serve.

Seezungen in Tomatensauce
(Soles in Tomato Sauce.)

For 6 Persons.   *Time of Preparation: 1½ hour.*

| 3½ lbs. soles. | 1½ pint tomato sauce. |

Clean and skin the soles (for skinning, see recipe "Boiled Sole"). Cut up into medium-sized pieces. Make a tomato sauce (see recipe). Place the pieces of sole in the sauce, steam for 10 minutes and serve.

Fisch in Tomatensauce
(Fish in Tomato Sauce.)

For 8 Persons.　　　　*Time of Preparation:* 1½ to 2. hours

4 lbs. fish (haddock, pike, perch, fresh herring, cod, tench).
1¼ lb. tomatoes.
6 oz. onions.
3 oz. butter.
2 oz. flour.

1 teaspoonful Liebig's Meat Extract, dissolved in 1½ pint water.
1 teaspoonful sugar.
1 tablespoonful lemon juice.
A pinch of pepper.
1 tablespoonful chopped parsley.

Well clean the fish, dry it and cut into medium-sized pieces.

Melt the butter in a saucepan and add to it the chopped onions. When they have been in the butter for 3 minutes, strew in the flour and then the tomatoes, cut into slices, and the water in which the Meat Extract has been dissolved

Let all boil gently for ¾ hour. Then pass through a sieve, and flavour with salt, sugar, pepper and lemon juice.

Place the pieces of fish in this sauce and boil them in it for 5 minutes. Then stir in the chopped parsley and serve.

Fisch in Fricassee-Sauce
Fish suitable for this dish are: Eel, haddock, pike, perch, fresh herring, tench and cod.

Make a white sauce (*see* recipe). Clean and cut up the fish, and boil for about 5 minutes in the white sauce till done, with 2 teaspoonsful of chopped onions and a pinch of pepper. Flavour the sauce with lemon juice and stir into it 3 yolks of eggs.

A few capers and mushrooms boiled in the sauce improve this dish, or a gill of Rhine wine or Moselle, flavouring the sauce in this latter case with lemon juice, 3 chopped Sardellen and a pinch of cayenne.

The dish may be garnished with little heaps of various vegetables arranged round it, such as cauliflower, asparagus, or Brussels sprouts, merely boiled in salt water.

Karpfen in Biersance
(Carp in Beer Sauce.)

For 6 Persons.　　　　*Time of Preparation:* 1 hour.

3 lbs. carp.

1 quart Polish beer sauce.

Scrape the scales off thoroughly, cut out the gills, and before cutting open the fish, wash it well and dry it with a cloth. Then place it on a board, cut off the fins, shorten the tail, cut the fish open and remove all the entrails careful-ly, so that the gall does not break. Only the gall and the thickest intestine are thrown away— the other portions are boiled with the fish; neither they nor the inside of the fish itself must be washed, or the special carp flavour will be lost. Now cut up the fish into medium-sized pieces, splitting open the head. Strew salt over them and stand, covered over, in a cool place for an hour.

Make a Polish sauce (see recipe). Place the fish in it, the head at the bottom, and boil it in this sauce. When it has boiled up once, taste the sauce, to see if it need the addition of any more salt.

In making the sauce, half the quantity of beer may be taken, red wine being substituted for the other half, or wine be altogether substituted for the beer.

Bream, tench and roach may be prepared in like manner, but must be completely cleaned, both inside and out.

(Sea Fish in Beer Sauce.)

Sea fish taste excellent if cooked in beer sauce, according to previous reci-pe, but after cutting them up, put them on to boil in cold water, strongly salt-ed. When the water just boils, take the fish out and finish boiling it in the beer sauce, the heads being removed altogether.

Gurnet should be scalded and skinned before being boiled in the beer sauce.

Aal-Grün
(Fresh Eel in White Sauce.)

For 6 persons.   *Time of Preparation:* 1½ hour.

2½ lbs. eel.	1 quart white sauce.
2 tablespoonsful lemon juice.	1 tablespoonful chopped parsley or
1 teaspoonful chopped onions.	dill.

Cut the eel into medium-sized pieces; make a white sauce (*see* recipe) and boil the eel in it with the chopped onion and a very little salt, till the flesh easily parts from the bones. Then add the chopped parsley or dill, flavour with lemon juice and serve.

Geraucherter Aal in Beer
(Smoked Eel in Beer.)

For 6 persons.   *Time of Preparation:* 1 hour.

1¾ lb. smoked eel.	1½ pint Polish beer sauce.

Brush the smoked eel well in lukewarm water, then rinse it well and cut it into medium-sized pieces and let it simmer for 10 minutes in a Polish beer sauce (*see* recipe), which must be well flavoured with lemon juice.

Aal in Weissbier

(Eel in Weissbier.)

For 6 Persons.   *Time of Preparation:* 1½ hour.

2 lbs. eel.	1 leaf sage.
1½ pint Weissbier.	A few peppercorns.
3 oz. butter.	Some lemon juice.
3 oz. flour.	½ teaspoonful sugar.
2 oz. onions.	Salt.
1 oz. parsley root.	

Brown the butter and flour in a saucepan to a golden colour. Add the Weissbier, the onions, cut into thin slices, some parsley root, a few peppercorns, a leaf of sage and a little salt, and boil well for 15 minutes. Then strain this sauce through a sieve and add to it the eel, cut into pieces, boiling until the flesh easily parts from the bones.

Flavour with lemon juice, salt, and half a teaspoonful of sugar and serve.

Gedämpfter Aal
(Stewed Eel.)

Boil 2 chopped-up calves' feet till the bones fall out. Then strain the broth off through a sieve and pour back into the saucepan. Place in it the eel, cut into pieces. Do not quite cover the eel with the broth and add 2 tablespoonsful of vinegar, in which ½ teaspoonful Meat Extract is dissolved, a little mace, 2 to 3 small onions cut into slices, pepper, salt, and a few slices of lemon. Cover the saucepan well, and stew very gently till the eel is tender. Serve the eel arranged in the centre of the dish, with the broth poured over it.

Gebackener Aal
(Fried and Baked Eel.)

Roll the pieces of eel in salt, egg, and breadcrumb, and fry a golden brown in butter, with fresh sage leaves.

Or, bake in the oven, rolled round and skewered with a wooden skewer, in a buttered pan with fresh herbs and slices of onion, and partly covered with equal quantities of white wine and vinegar. When the eel is done, place on a cloth, for the fat to be absorbed, draw out the skewers, brush over with glaze and serve with tomato sauce.

Aal in pikanter Kräutersauce
(Eel in Piquant Herb Sauce.)

For 6 Persons.　　　　　*Time of Preparation:* 1½ hour.

2 lbs. eel.	4 teaspoonsful chopped onions.
1½ pint white sauce.	2 teaspoonsful chopped parsley.
1 gill Rhine wine.	1 teaspoonsful chopped dill.
1 gill vinegar.	1 teaspoonsful chopped chives.
1¾ pint water.	1 teaspoonsful chopped Liebig's
6 yolks of eggs.	Meat Extract.

Bring to the boil 1¾ pint water and 1 gill of vinegar. Clean and cut up the eel and place it in the boiling dilute vinegar, boil up once again, then take out the eel and place it on a sieve to drain.

Make 1½ pint white sauce (*see* recipe), place the eel in it, with the chopped onion and some salt, and boil till the flesh easily parts from the bones. Then take out and place on a china dish, keeping it warm, while the preparation of the sauce is completed.

Add to the latter the wine, lemon juice. Meat Extract, the chopped dill, chives, and parsley, and finally the 6 yolks, stirring briskly till the sauce boils. Then pour over the eel and serve.

This method of preparation is also to be recommended for haddock, gurnet, and perch.

Chopped mushrooms may be substituted for the chives, dill and parsley, if preferred.

Fisch-Frikassee
(Fricassee of Fish.)

For 8 Persons.　　　　　*Time of Preparation:* 3 hours.

3 lbs. fish (haddock, pike, perch, etc.).	2 oz. soup herbs (parsley root, carrots, turnips, celery).
20 crayfish.	2 oz. chopped onions.
1¼ lb. calves' sweetbread.	A few peppercorns.
2 oz. mushrooms.	½ teaspoonful Meat Extract.
6 oz. butter.	3½ pints water.
3 oz. flour.	A little lemon juice.
3 Sardellen.	Salt.
6 yolks of eggs.	Some capers.
	Slices of lemon.

Boil the sweetbreads for 40 minutes in the water with salt, a few peppercorns, 2 oz. soup herbs. For the last 10 minutes add the fish. Remove the bones and skin from the fish. With half a pound of the fish make fish balls (*see* recipe), and boil them in the broth for a few minutes. With the crayfish, flour, butter and broth make a crayfish sauce (*see* recipe). Add to it the mushrooms, chopped fine, and stir into it half a teaspoonful of Meat Extract. Flavour with lemon juice and the Sardellen, chopped fine, and finally stir in the 6 yolks. Garnish the dish with the tails of the crayfish, the remaining fish balls, slices of lemon, capers, and a few quite small crayfish.

Fisch-Ragoat
(Fish Ragout.)

For 12 Scallop Shells.

2½ lbs. filleted fish (haddock, pike or perch).	¾ pint water, in which about a teaspoonful Liebig's Meat Extract is dissolved.
6 oz. butter.	
2 tablespoonsful lemon juice.	1 teaspoonful chopped onions.
1 oz. flour.	3 teaspoonsful capers.
1 gill white wine.	2 oz. grated Parmesan cheese.
Pepper and salt.	

Skin and fillet the fish and cut into dice about half an inch square. Sprinkle them over with salt and pepper and lemon juice and stand in a cool place for lo minutes.

Melt 3 oz. of the butter in a saucepan, put into it the fish and shake the saucepan to and fro till the fish is done. Then stand on one side.

Brown the flour with an oz. of butter to a golden colour. Add the chopped onions, then gradually the water in which the Meat Extract has been dissolved, stirring well, and bring to the boil. Then add the capers, and lastly the 6 yolks beaten up with the white wine. Into this sauce stir the fish.

Take 12 scallop shells. Butter them well, cover the bottom of each with a layer of grated roll and then fill with the ragout. Sprinkle with a little grated Parmesan cheese, melt the remainder of the butter and pour it over each shell. Bake in a hot oven 10 to 15 minutes.

The addition of chopped mushrooms to the ragout is an improvement.

Geschmorter Fisch
(Stewed Fish.)

For 6 Persons.   *Time of Preparation:* 1½ hour.
Perch, Pike, Haddock, Cod, etc.

3 lbs. fish.	1 gill sour cream.
4 oz. butter.	1 teaspoonful chopped onion.
1 oz. flour.	1 teaspoonful chopped parsley.
1 gill water, in which ½ teaspoonful of Liebig's Meat Extract is dissolved.	1 sage leaf.
	A pinch of pepper.

1 tablespoonful salt.

For cod and haddock allow a larger quantity, say 3½ lbs.

Clean the fish well, removing' the scales. Cut into medium-sized pieces and place in a covered pan for half an hour with onions, herbs, pepper and salt. Then brown the butter in a saucepan, dredge the pieces of fish with flour and place them in the butter. Leave them in it for 5 minutes, then add the stock, made by dissolving the Meat Extract in a gill of water, and the cream, thickened with a teaspoonful of flour, and leave the fish stewing in this sauce until done.

With haddock and cod, pour the stock and cream at once over the fish, instead of leaving it in the brown butter for 5 minutes first.

White wine may be substituted for the sour cream.

Flunder oder Knurrhahn gedämpft
(Stewed Plaice or Gurnet.)

For 8 *Persons.*   *Time of Preparation:* 2 hours

4½ lbs. fish.	2 tablespoonsful lemon juice.
1 pint brown sauce.	1 teaspoonful chopped parsley.
½ pint red wine.	½ teaspoonful chopped Liebig's
3 Sardellen.	Meat Extract.
5 oz. salt.	A little sugar.

Clean and skin the fish, cut it into medium-sized pieces, sprinkle it with salt, pour over it the lemon juice and stand in a cool place for an hour.

Make a brown sauce (*see* recipe). Place the fish in it in a covered saucepan, with the red wine. Meat Extract, a little sugar and the chopped onions. Bring to the boil, then draw aside and stew slowly for 10 minutes. Add finally the chopped Sardellen and serve.

Gespickter Fisch
(Larded Fish.)

Pike, Perch or Haddock.
For 6 *Persons.*   *Time of Preparation:* 21 hours.

3 lbs. fish.	2 tablespoonsful lemon juice.
2 oz. bacon.	2 tablespoonsful Parmesan cheese.
4 oz. butter.	1 gill Liebig's Meat Extract stock.
1 oz. flour.	½ pint cream.
1 oz. salt.	Some breadcrumbs.
1 bacon rind.	1 teaspoonful pepper.

Clean and scale the fish. Make a slit along the back and rub the fish well over with salt.

Cut the bacon into fine strips, roll them in pepper and salt, and lard the fish with them on both sides. Then pour the lemon juice over the fish and stand it in a cool place for an hour.

After this, place it on a piece of bacon rind in a baking-tin, pour over it some of the stock (made by dissolving the Meat Extract in a gill of water), and put into a very hot oven, basting frequently with hot browned butter and adding from time to time alternately a little stock and the cream, thickened with an oz. of flour.

When done, sprinkle with grated Parmesan cheese and breadcrumbs, then pour over a little browned butter and leave a few minutes in the oven to get brown before serving.

Gerichte aus gehacktem Fischfleisch
(Dishes prepared with Minced Fish.)

Fischklösse I.
(Fish Balls I.)

1¼ lb. fish (without bones or skin).
½ pint cream.
A few peppercorns.
Soup herbs (carrots, turnips, celery, parsley root).

2 teaspoonsful salt.
A pinch of pepper.
An onion.

3¼ lbs. of fresh haddock yield on the average 1¼ lb. of fish when freed from skin and bones.

Skin and fillet the fish, dry it well with a cloth, pass it through the mincing machine twice and then pound it in a mortar. Rub it through a hair sieve next and then pound again, adding during the pounding the cream which has been first whipped until very stiff. Form into little balls.

In the meanwhile the bones and skin should have been put on to boil with an onion, carrots, celery, parsley root, and a few peppercorns. In a quart of the broth so obtained, which must be boiling, throw the fish balls and let them boil gently for 4 minutes.

Fischklösse II.
(Fish Balls II.)

¾ lb. fish (without bones or skin).
2 oz. fresh butter.
1 egg.

A pinch of pepper.
A pinch of salt.
A pinch of cayenne

Prepare the fish as in last recipe and pound it for one hour in a mortar, adding during the process salt, pepper, cayenne, fresh butter and a beaten-up egg. Then rub through a hair sieve, form into balls, and boil as in preceding recipe.

Fischklösschen für Frikassees
(Fish Balls for Fricassees.)

2 oz. butter.	1 lb. fish (without bones or skin).
1 egg.	1 oz. breadcrumbs.
A pinch of pepper.	A pinch of salt.

Prepare the fish and pound thoroughly in a mortar, according to recipe I.

Cream the butter, add to it the breadcrumbs, salt, pepper, a beaten-up egg and the pounded fish and stir well for ID minutes to a stiff paste.

Spread this paste about ½-inch thick on a china plate and cut out from it with a teaspoon (which must be dipped each time in boiling water) little rounds, which are then boiled in the fish broth for 3 minutes.

Fischklösse im Reisring
(Fish Balls in a Ring of Rice.)

Prepare the fish balls according to either of the preceding recipes. Boil them in salt water and place them to keep warm in a basin standing in hot water.

Then prepare a tomato sauce (*see* recipe), using in its preparation some of the water in which the fish balls have been boiled.

Scald 6 oz. rice and boil it slowly with 1¼ pint of the fish-ball water, 4 oz. butter, an onion and salt to taste. When the rice is quite soft, remove the onion and fill a ring-shaped mould, pressing the rice into it firmly. Turn out upon a dish and fill the centre of the ring with the tomato sauce and fish balls.

Fisch-Pudding.
(Fish Pudding.)

For 6 Persons.	*Time of Preparation:* 3 hours.

1¾ lb. fish (without bones or skin).	2 oz. breadcrumbs,
4 whites of eggs.	1½ oz. grated Parmesan cheese
4 oz. butter.	3 whole eggs.
1 teaspoonful finely chopped pars-	4 yolks of eggs
ley.	A pinch each of pepper and salt.
1 teaspoonful finely chopped onion.	

Chop the fish well and pass it several times through the mincing machine. Then pound it in a mortar. Stir 2 oz. breadcrumbs, 3 beaten-up eggs, 1 oz.

butter well in a saucepan till they become a dough-like mass; then remove from the fire and stir in the chopped onion. When cool, add 3 oz. butter which has been creamed, the 4 yolks of eggs, parsley, salt, pepper, the grated Parmesan cheese and the pounded fish. Mix very thoroughly and then stir in the 4 whites of eggs, whisked stiffly. Put into a well-buttered mould and steam for 1½ hour. Turn out and serve with Sardellen, Caper, Oyster, Caviar or Fricassee Sauce. (*See* the various recipes, under section "Sauces.")

Fisch-Hackbraten
(Fish Cake.)

For 6 Persons.   *Time of Preparation:* 3½ hours.

¾lb. fish (without bones or skin).	1 teaspoonful chopped onions.
1 oz. breadcrumbs.	½ pint sour cream.
4 whole eggs.	½ pint water in which ½ teaspoon-
2 yolks of eggs.	ful Liebig's Meat Extract has been
1 slice of fat bacon.	dissolved.
3 oz. butter.	A pinch of salt.
1 oz. flour.	pepper.
2 oz. finely chopped bacon.	1 teaspoonful German mustard.

Mix 1 oz. of the breadcrumbs with ½ oz. butter and 2 eggs. Stir well in a saucepan until they become a dough-like mass; then remove from the fire and stir in the chopped onion. Place in a basin and when cool, add the remaining 2 eggs and the 2 extra yolks, well-beaten, ½ oz. flour, the mustard, the finely-chopped fish and bacon, and a pinch each of salt and pepper. Mix thoroughly and then form into the shape of a long loaf. Brush over with egg, roll in breadcrumbs, and place on a slice of fat bacon in a baking-pan. Baste with hot, browned butter, and bake, adding from time to time a little of the ½ pint of water in which the Meat Extract has been dissolved, and finally, the cream, thickened with ½ oz. flour.

This is excellent with salad, cauliflower, green peas, Brussels sprouts and potato dishes.

Gebackener Fisch
(*Baked Fish.*)

Fisch in der Form gebacken
(Fish Baked in a Mould.)

Pike, Perch, Haddock, Cod.
For 6 Persons.   *Time of Preparation:* 1½ hour.

3 lbs. fish.	5 oz. butter.

2 oz. chopped Sardellen.	2 tablespoonsful grated Parmesan
Lemon juice.	cheese.
Breadcrumbs.	1 tablespoonful capers.
	1 tablespoonful chopped fresh herbs.

Butter a mould well and fill it with the fish, which has been first boiled in strongly salted water, then filleted and cut into medium-sized pieces. Place between the layers of fish the chopped fresh herbs, capers and chopped Sardellen and a little pepper. Melt the butter and pour it over and sprinkle grated Parmesan cheese and breadcrumbs on the top. Finally add the juice of a lemon and bake in a hot oven for 15 minutes.

Seezunge in einer Schüssel gebacken
(Baked Sole.)

For 8 *Persons.*   *Time of Preparation:* 2 hours.

4½ lbs. soles.	1 tablespoonful chopped fresh herbs.
2 oz. breadcrumbs.	3 tablespoonsful chopped mush-
1 shallot chopped fine.	rooms.
4 oz. butter.	Lemon juice.
1 gill white wine.	A pinch of pepper.
1 gill stock.	

Clean and skin the soles and cut up into medium-sized pieces. Rub them over with salt, and sprinkle over them the shallot, chopped fine, and a little lemon juice, and stand in a cool place for ½ hour.

Butter a mould and line it with the finely-chopped fresh herbs. Place the fish upon these and cover with a layer of chopped mushrooms and the rest of the herbs, putting little lumps of butter on the top. Pour over the wine and stock, then put on a top layer of breadcrumbs and bake in a hot oven for half an hour.

Gebackener Fisch mit Blumenkohl
(*Baked Fish with Cauliflower.*)

Pike, Tench or Haddock.

For 6 *Persons.*   *Time of Preparation:* 2½ hours.

2 lbs. fish.	1 tablespoonful grated Parmesan
2 lbs. potatoes.	cheese.
4 oz. butter.	1 tablespoonful breadcrumbs.
1 oz. flour.	A pinch of pepper.
½ pint sour cream.	Salt.
1 lb. cauliflower.	Soup herbs.

Boil the fish with soup herbs (carrots, celery, parsley root, etc.), let it cool, then cut into medium-sized pieces, removing bones and skin.

Boil 2 lbs. of potatoes, cutting into slices when cold. Boil some small cauliflowers and put them on a sieve to drain.

Heat 1 oz. flour and 2 oz. butter in a saucepan to a golden brown, then add gradually the cream and the stock. Boil this sauce for 3 minutes, flavouring with pepper and salt to taste, and strain.

Butter a mould and place in it alternate layers of fish, cauliflower and potatoes, pouring the remaining 2 oz. of butter (oiled) over the cauliflower and potatoes. Over the whole of it pour the sauce and sprinkle grated Parmesan cheese and breadcrumbs on the top. Bake in a hot oven.

The addition of boiled calves' sweetbreads or brains is an improvement to this dish. Macaroni or Nudeln (see recipe, page 18) may be substituted for the potatoes and cauliflower.

Kalte Fisch-Gerichte
(Cold Fish Dishes.)

Fische in Gelee.
(Fish in Aspic.)
Gurnet, Pike, Eel, Salmon, Haddock.

For 6 Persons.   *Time of Preparation:* 1½ hour.

2 lbs. eel or salmon (of the other fish reckon 3 lbs.).	Soup herbs (carrots, celery, parsley root).
2½ pints vegetable stock.	½ pint best vinegar.
1 oz. gelatine.	3 oz. onions.
	A few peppercorns.

Clean the fish well, cut it up into medium-sized pieces and boil till done in water in which soup herbs have been previously boiled, with plenty of salt, some peppercorns and vinegar.

Remove the bones from the fish when cooked, and arrange in a well-buttered mould. Add gelatine to the stock, reckoning 1 oz. to every quart of stock. Clear the latter with white of egg and eggshells and strain through a cloth on to the fish in the mould. The addition of a little Meat Extract is an improvement. Salmon in aspic with green peas is an excellent dish and looks attractive. The green peas are placed in the aspic between the layers of fish, the aspic being allowed to set before the next layer of fish is put in.

Lachs als kalte Schüssel
(Salmon Whole, with Aspic)

Clean the fish well, tie a cloth round it, and just bring it to the boil in slightly salted water with a little vinegar. Then pour away this water and boil the fish in vegetable stock, as in last recipe. The substitution of Rhine wine for the vinegar is an improvement.

Leave the fish in the stock to cool, then take it out and place on a large dish. Make an aspic of the stock (*see* last recipe), clear it with egg shells, and brush the salmon over with it.

Garnish the dish with little heaps of various vegetables, slices of hard-boiled eggs, crayfish, lobster, and the chopped-up aspic.

Aal entgrätet in Aspic
(Filleted Eel in Aspic.)

Skin the eel, cut off head and tail, slit it up along the back, and remove the backbone, being careful not to injure the gall, which must be removed unbroken. Then clean the eel well. Cut a small eel lengthways into two strips; with a large eel, cut each of these strips again in two, lengthwise.

Sprinkle each strip with finely-chopped fresh herbs, salt and pepper, roll up firmly and tie round with string. Put each little roll into a piece of muslin, tieing up again with string, and boil in aspic (*see* recipe, p. 41) for about half an hour.

Then place the rolls between two boards, and press them well. Remove muslin and string, cut into slices, and place in aspic, or serve with Remouladen Sauce (see recipe) poured over them.

The dish may be garnished with slices of hard-boiled eggs, or cucumber, crayfish, etc.

Gerichte aus Fischresten
(*Dishes prepared with Cooked Fish.*)

Pannfisch.

For 6 Persons.   *Time of Preparation:* 1 hour.

1 lb. cold boiled fish.	A pinch of pepper.
2 lbs. boiled potatoes.	½ pint cream.
3 oz. butter.	3½ oz. chopped onions.
A tablespoonful salt.	

Boil the potatoes and cut into slices when cold.

Brown the butter and heat the chopped onion in it. Sprinkle salt over the sliced potatoes, and fry them a golden brown in the butter. Pick the fish apart, dust it over with pepper and add it and the cream to the potatoes. Let all boil up and serve on a very hot dish, garnished with slices of pickled cucumbers (saure Gurken).

Fisch in Muscheln gereicht
(Fish in Scallops.)

For 12 Scallop Shells.   *Time of Preparation:* 1½ hour.

1 lb. cold boiled fish.	1½ pint strong white sauce.
6 oz. butter.	1 tablespoonful lemon juice.
1 lb. tinned asparagus tips.	1 tablespoonful chopped parsley.
2 oz. grated Parmesan cheese.	6 yolks of eggs.

Make a white sauce (*see* recipe). Put into it the parsley, lemon juice, and capers, then stir in the yolks of eggs, the picked fish and asparagus tips. Brush over the shells with oiled butter, put in a layer of grated Parmesan cheese, and fill with the mixture. Cover with another layer of cheese, melt the butter, and pour some over each scallop. Bake 15 minutes in a hot oven.

Fisch mit Rührei
(Fish with Scrambled Eggs.)

For 6 Persons.   *Time of Preparation*: ½ hour.

1 lb. boiled fish.	½ tablespoonful chopped onions.
6 eggs.	½ tablespoonful capers.
2 oz. butter.	2 tablespoonful water in which very
1 tablespoonful salt.	little Liebig's Meat Extract has been
A pinch of pepper.	dissolved.
1 tablespoonful chopped parsley.	

Brown the butter, then add the onion and the picked fish and fry for 3 minutes, shaking the pan continually. Beat the eggs well with the capers, salt, pepper, lemon juice, parsley and 2 tablespoonsful of the Meat Extract stock, and pour over the fish. Stir well over a brisk fire till the eggs are scrambled, but not too firm, and serve on a very hot dish. Sprinkle over with chopped parsley and surround with little roasted potatoes.

Hering
(Herring Dishes.)

Salzheringe in weisser Sauce
(Pickled Herrings in White Sauce.)

3 tablespoonsful oil.	3 oz. onions cut into slices
1 tablespoonful German mustard.	1½ pint vinegar.
1 oz. flour.	1 gill water.
A pinch of ground ginger.	A few peppercorns
15 herrings.	A pinch of cayenne.

Take 15 pickled herrings (obtainable at any German Delikatessen shop). Soak them for 24 hours, then clean and scale them well, removing the heads, and wash them in fresh water.

Stir the oil and flour together over a brisk fire for a few minutes, add the water, and boil up well. Pour into an earthen vessel, adding gradually the vinegar (which has been boiled with sliced onion) and when cool, the roes of the herrings, chopped fine.

Rub the sauce so obtained through a fine sieve and flavour with German mustard, ground ginger, cayenne and small boiled onions. Place the herrings in a stone jar, pour this sauce over them and tie up the jar. The addition of a little chopped apple and thick cream to the sauce, on serving, is a great improvement.

Rollmops
(Rolled Herring.)

Soak the pickled herrings for 24 hours, cut them lengthwise into two strips, removing bones and skin. Cover each strip with a layer of capers, chopped onions, German mustard and slices of pickled cucumber.

Roll up and fasten together with a fine wooden skewer.

Place these little rolls in a stone jar and pour over them vinegar that has been boiled with onions and allowed to cool. Tie up the jars till the herrings are required.

Delikatess-Heringe
(Piquant Herring.)

15 fresh herrings.	1 teaspoonful sugar.
1 gill best vinegar.	A very little Meat Extract.
A little pepper.	Mustard seed (Senfkörner).
Some sliced onion.	Tarragon vinegar to taste.
1 tablespoonful salt.	

Fillet the herrings. Dry the fillets with a cloth and lay them in glass jars, pouring wine vinegar over them and leaving them to stand for 36 hours. Then pour off the vinegar, strew salt, pepper, sugar, and mustard seeds among the herrings, and stand in a cool place for another 3 hours. Boil up the gill of vinegar with the sliced onions, dissolve a little Meat Extract in it and, when it is cool, pour it over the herrings. Add a little Tarragon vinegar to taste, or a teaspoonful of German mustard, or slices of tomatoes.

Tie up the jars and stand them in a cool place. The herrings are ready for use in 3 days.

Frische Heringe marimert
(Marinaded Fresh Herrings.)

Scale and clean the herrings, cutting off the heads. Wash them well and lay them in salt for 2 hours, reckoning 2 oz. salt to every 15 herrings. Then dry them, roll them in flour, and fry in browned butter. Place in a stone jar with a few peppercorns and pour over them boiled vinegar that has been allowed to cool.

Sardellen-Torte
(Sardellen Entrée.)

1 lb. Sardellen.	1 tablespoonful chopped green herbs.
4 oz. Parmesan cheese.	
4 oz. butter.	1 tablespoonful capers.
1 small toast loaf.	2 tablespoonsful lemon juice.

Cut the bread into slices, removing crusts, and toast it. Butter a dish well and place the pieces of toast on it. Put a layer of grated Parmesan cheese on each piece of toast, and on that arrange the Sardellen, which have been pre-viously soaked in milk, strewing over them a few capers and the chopped herbs. Then pour the lemon juice over and the butter, which has in the meanwhile been oiled; on the top, sprinkle another layer of Parmesan cheese and bake in a hot oven for about 10 minutes.

Serve as an entrée.

Krebse.
(Crayfish.)

In buying crayfish, care should be taken that the tails are curved in. Should the tails be stretched out straight, the crayfish are dead. The same applies to lobsters. If the crayfish do not appear clean, they should be cleansed by brushing and then well washed.

To boil a dozen crayfish reckon from 1 to 2 quarts of water, according to size. They must boil lo to 15 minutes slowly, and then be drawn to one side to simmer slowly for another quarter of an hour.

To each quart of water add 1 oz. of salt, a few carraway seeds, a small onion, and some parsley. Let the water boil briskly before throwing in the live crayfish and throw each in separately, letting the water boil up again before the next be thrown in. To throw all in at once sends the water off the boil for some time and, thus preventing instant death, is an unnecessary cruelty.

When the crayfish are boiled, serve in a tureen with some of the broth in which they have been boiled, to which a little fresh butter has been added, or the following sauce may be handed with them.

1 gill of the crayfish broth.	1 tablespoonful chopped parsley.
1 gill water, in which ½ teaspoonful	1 teaspoonful chopped dill.
Liebig's Meat Extract is dissolved.	2 oz. butter.
1 oz. breadcrumbs,	

Melt the butter, stir the breadcrumbs into it, add the broth and the Meat Extract stock and boil for about 5 minutes. Then add the chopped parsley and dill. The meat may be extracted from the crayfish and served in scallop shells, the sauce being poured over them.

Hummer-Frikassee
(Lobster Fricassee.)

For 6 Persons.   *Time of Preparation:* 1 hour.

1 lb. tinned lobster.	1 oz. flour.
½ lb. tinned asparagus tips.	1 oz. butter.
¼ lb. bottled mushrooms.	6 yolks of eggs.
1 lb. calves' sweetbreads.	3 tablespoonsful white wine.
1¼ pint stock.	4 tablespoonsful chopped parsley
Soup herbs (carrots, celery, parsley	mixed with a little dill.
root, etc.).	Lemon juice.
1 Sardelle.	

Boil the stock well with the soup herbs, cut up small, then add the sweetbreads and boil for another 40 minutes. Turn the asparagus tips out on to a sieve to drain: add a tablespoonful of the water out of the tin to the broth.

Turn out the mushrooms and drain them in like manner, also adding to the broth a tablespoonful of the water they were in.

Cut up the mushrooms into small pieces. Divide the lobster into suitable pieces, slice up the sweetbread and warm up lobster, sweetbread, asparagus, and mushrooms on a sieve placed over boiling water.

With ½ pint of the stock, the butter and flour make a brown sauce (*see* recipe) and flavour it with the Sardelle, chopped fine, lemon juice, wine, chopped parsley and dill. Then stir into it the 6 yolks. Put the warmed-up lobster, etc., into this sauce and serve garnished with little crescents of puff paste. Some of the lobster and asparagus may be reserved as an additional garnish.

Austern-Ragout.
(Oyster Ragout.)

For 6 Persons.   *Time of Preparation:* 2 hours.

3 doz. oysters.	Lemon juice.
1½ pint stock.	Pepper.
1 gill white wine.	Salt.
1 oz. flour.	Soup herbs (carrots, celery, parsley
1 oz. butter.	root, etc.).
6 yolks of eggs.	An onion.
1 lb. calves' sweetbreads.	

Boil the sweetbread with the onion and soup herbs in the stock. When it has boiled for 20 minutes, mix the butter and flour to a stiff paste and put it into the stock, which should boil for another 15 minutes slowly. Then take out the sweetbread and cut it into dice. Add the wine to the stock to make a sauce, strain through a fine sieve, flavour with pepper and plenty of lemon juice, boil up again, beat the yolks of eggs well with some of the oyster liquor and stir into the sauce.

Beard the oysters, add them with the sweetbread to the sauce and serve. Garnish the dish with oyster shells.

Tinned oysters may be used for this dish.

Saucen
(*Sauces.*)

Weisse Grundsauce.
(White Sauce.)

For 6 Persons.   *Time of Preparation:* 1 hour.

2 oz. butter.	2 tablespoonsful chopped soup
2 oz. flour.	1 onion. herbs.
1½ pint stock.	A little spice and salt.

Heat the butter and flour together to a pale golden colour, then, stirring continually, add first some of the stock cold and then the rest of the stock hot, and bring to the boil, still stirring continually. Then add all the other ingredients and stand the sauce on one side to simmer for a quarter of an hour. Strain through a hair sieve and use as the groundwork to many different kinds of sauces.

Braune Grundsauce
(Brown Sauce.)

The same ingredients as above, except that 3 oz. of flour are taken and the flour and butter are heated till of a dark brown colour. This and the previous sauce are used in making nearly all the following sauces, and are referred to as "white" or "brown" sauces.

Herings-Sauce
(Herring Sauce.)

For 6 Persons.   *Time of Preparation:* 1 hour.

1½ pint white sauce.	2 herrings.
Lemon juice.	Salt.

Fillet the herrings, lay them in water for 2 hours, chop finely and add to the white sauce, which has been warmed in the meantime, but must not be allowed to boil any longer. The sauce should, just before serving, be flavoured with lemon juice to taste. It is improved by the addition of 2 tablespoonsful of cream.

Sardellen-Sauce

For 6 Persons.   *Time of Preparation:* 1 hour.

1½ pint white sauce.	4 oz. Sardellen.
2 shallots.	1 oz. butter.

Remove the bones from the Sardellen. Boil these bones in the white sauce, then strain and add the fish and shallots, both chopped finely, and the butter.

Tomaten-Sauce
(Tomato Sauce.)

For 6 Persons.   *Time of Preparation:* 1 hour.

1½ pints white or brown sauce.	1 oz. butter.
1 oz. raw smoked ham.	A little lemon juice.
¾ lb. tomatoes.	

Make 1½ pints of white or brown sauce and boil in it for 15 minutes the tomatoes cut into slices, the ham, chopped finely, and a little lemon juice. Pass through a sieve and then stir in the butter.

Champignon-Sauce
(Mushroom Sauce.)

For 6 Persons.　　　　　　　　*Time of Preparation:* 1 hour.

1½ pint white sauce.	1 oz. raw smoked ham.
4 oz. mushrooms.	¾ oz. butter.
The yolk of 1 egg.	A little lemon juice.

Make 1½ pint of white sauce, strain it, boil up in it the mushrooms, finely chopped, with the smokedham, also finely chopped, and flavour with lemon juice. Then stir in the butter and finally the yolk of 1 egg.

Frikassee-Sauce
(Fricassee Sauce.)

For 6 Persons.　　　　　　　　*Time of Preparation:* 1 hour.

1½ pint white sauce.	1 teaspoonful capers.
3 Sardellen.	Yolks of 3 eggs.
1 oz. butter.	1 tablespoonful Rhine wine.
6 champignons.	A little lemon juice.

Remove the bones from the Sardellen, chop the latter finely, prepare and cut up the champignons. Put both into the white sauce and boil up. Flavour with lemon juice and the wine, stir in the butter and just before serving, the yolks of eggs.

Bechamel-Sauce

For 6 Persons.　　　　　　　　*Time of Preparation:* 1 hour.

3 oz. flour.	3 oz. chopped onions.
2 oz. butter.	1 oz. finely chopped ham.
1 pint stock.	Salt.
1 pint cream.	

Put the onions and 2 oz. butter into a saucepan. When the onions are transparent, strew in the flour, and when the latter is a delicate golden colour add the chopped ham and stock, stirring well. Boil for 10 minutes, then strain through a sieve and stir in an additional oz. of butter and the cream which has been meanwhile brought to the boil.

Should the sauce be served with potatoes, half the quantity of flour should be taken.

This sauce may be greatly improved by the addition of about 3 table-spoonsful of roast chicken, turkey or veal, pounded in a mortar, the sauce being further flavoured with lemon juice and 4 pounded sweet almonds. This variation of the sauce is excellent with fish and chicken.

Meerrettig-Sauce
(Horseradish Sauce.)

For 6 Persons.   *Time of Preparation*: 1 hour.

1 pint white sauce.	½ a medium-sized horseradish.
2 oz. butter.	A pinch of nutmeg.

Peel the horseradish, moisten it with vinegar, then grate it, pouring a little milk or lemon juice on it to prevent it becoming blue.

Make a white sauce and, when boiling, stir in the grated nutmeg with 2 oz. butter. The sauce must not be allowed to continue boiling, or it loses its flavour. If cream instead of stock be used to make the white sauce, the horseradish sauce is much improved.

Mandelmeerrettig
(Horseradish Sauce with Almonds.)

6 oz. almonds.	Butter the size of an egg.
A little cream.	A thick stick of horseradish.
1 tablespoonful flour.	

Scrape and grate a thick stick of horseradish. Blanch and grate 6 oz. almonds, and mix both with 1 tablespoonful flour, butter the size of an &%g, cream to make it the proper consistency for a sauce and stir over the fire till it thickens.

Krebs-Sauce
(Crayfish Sauce.)

For 6 Persons.   *Time of Preparation*: 1½ hour.

15 crayfish.	1½ pint stock.
2 oz. flour	1 Sardelle.
3 oz. butter.	3 yolks of eggs.
1 teaspoonful capers.	Lemon juice.

Brush the crayfish well and boil them 15 minutes in water with salt. Then break off the claws and tails, extracting the meat and taking out the "cream."

Remove the gray threads at the side, and the galls and entrails.

Pound up the shells in a mortar, melt the butter in a saucepan, put in the pounded shells and fry for 3 minutes; strew in the flour, fry another minute, stir in the stock and boil gently for quarter of an hour. Now strain through a wire sieve, add the capers and the Sardelle, finely chopped, lemon juice and salt to taste, stir in the yolks of eggs and the meat of the crayfish and serve.

This sauce is improved by the addition of chopped mushrooms.

It may be prepared equally well from lobster or shrimps.

Fisch-Sauce.
(Fish Sauce.)

For 6 Persons.   *Time of Preparation:* 1½ hour.

½ lb. fish.	2 tablespoonsful chopped soup
1 Sardelle.	herbs.
2 oz. butter.	1 tablespoonful Moselle.
2 oz. flour.	Yolks of 2 eggs.
2 oz. chopped onion.	1 bayleaf.
1½ pint stock.	Salt.
	A pinch of spice.

Clean the fish well and cut up into small pieces. Melt the butter, sprinkle in the flour, stirring till smooth. Add the chopped onion and fish, then pour in the stock and, lastly, the chopped soup herbs, the bayleaf, and a pinch of spice. Simmer for half an hour with the lid on. Then pass through a hair sieve, so that the bones are removed, and flavour with lemon juice, salt, the finely-chopped Sardelle and the wine. Finally, stir in the yolks of eggs.

This is a suitable sauce for Fish Fricassee, or Cauliflower, or Asparagus.

Austern-Sauce
(Oyster Sauce.)

For 6 Persons.   *Time of Preparation:* 1½ hour.

1 ½ pint fish sauce.	20 oysters.	Lemon juice.

Take the oysters out of their shells, removing the beards, and place them for a few minutes in lemon juice. Make 1½ pint of fish sauce (see previous recipe) and add the oysters to it just before serving.

Kaviar-Sauce
(Caviar Sauce.)

For 6 Persons.   *Time of Preparation:* 1½ hour.

1 lb. caviar. | 1½ pint fish sauce.

Prepare fish sauce according to recipe and stir in the caviar.
Ordinary melted butter may be made and the caviar added.

Gurken-Sauce.
(Cucumber Sauce.)

For 6 Persons.   *Time of Preparation:* 1 hour.

1½ pint brown sauce.	A little vinegar.
2 Salzgurken (salted gherkins).	Salt.
½ teaspoonful chopped onions.	Sugar.

Prepare 1½ pint of brown sauce. Peel the gherkins, cut them into slices and boil them with the onion in the sauce for 5 minutes, flavouring with vinegar, salt and sugar to taste. A few slices of apple may be added.

Trüffel-Sauce
(Truffle Sauce.)

1 oz. truffles.	¾ oz. butter.
1½ pint brown or white sauce.	½ teaspoonful Liebig's Meat Extract.
½ gill white wine.	

Peel the truffles and boil them well in the sauce, with the Meat Extract. Then take them out, cut them into small pieces, place them on again to simmer for 10 minutes in the wine, warmed with the butter in it, and then add the sauce.

If a white sauce has been used, the yolks of 2 eggs may be stirred in when the sauce boils up again.

Rotwein-Sauce
(Red Wine Sauce.)

For 6 Persons.   *Time of Preparation:* 1 hour.

½ pint red wine.	Sugar.
1 pint brown sauce.	2 finely chopped Sardellen.
2 oz. butter.	Half a bayleaf.
2 oz. chopped onion.	Parsley.
Salt.	

Put the red wine on to boil in an earthenware or enamel saucepan with the onion, parsley and bayleaf, and boil with the lid on till the quantity has been reduced to 3 tablespoonsful.

Then strain through a sieve, add the sauce (prepared from 1 pint of water in which fish has been boiled, and 1 pint of water in which a teaspoonful of Liebig's Meat Extract has been dissolved), flavour with the Sardelle and a little sugar and stir in the butter.

Suitable for carp, salmon and eel.

Burgunder-Sauce
(Burgundy Sauce.)

For 6 Persons.   *Time of Preparation:* 1¼ hour.

1½ pint thick brown sauce.	½ oz. sugar.
2 oz. small onions.	½ teaspoonful Meat Extract dis-
¼ pint Burgundy.	solved in ¼ pint water.

Peel the onions and scald them three times. Brown the sugar, add the lemon juice and a little stock (or broth formed by dissolving ½ teaspoonful of Meat Extract in ¼ pint of water) and stew the onions in it until they become transparent and brown.

Then add the brown sauce, boil all up again and add the Burgundy.

Madeira-Sauce

For 6 Persons.   *Time of Preparation:* 1 hour.

1½ pint brown sauce.	2 oz. butter.
½ teaspoonful sugar.	A little Liebig's Meat Extract.
½ teaspoonful chopped onion.	Lemon juice.

Madeira to taste.

Make 1½ pint of brown sauce. Add to it a little Meat Extract and the chopped onions and bring to the boil, stirring continuously. Flavour with sugar, lemon juice and Madeira to taste, and finally stir in 2 oz, butter.

Rosinen-Sauce
(Sultana Sauce.)

For 6 Persons.   *Time of Preparation:* 1 hour.

1½ pint brown sauce.	A pinch of pounded cloves.
¼lb. sultanas.	A pinch of allspice.
A pinch of cinnamon.	1 teaspoonful chopped onion.

½ teaspoonful lemon peel.
Lemon juice, salt and sugar to taste.

1 oz. sweet almonds.

Boil all ingredients in the brown sauce for 10 minutes, and flavour to taste with salt, sugar and lemon juice.

Polnische Sauce
(Polish Sauce.)

For 6 persons.   *Time of Preparation:* 1 hour.

1¼ pint brown beer.
½ oz. flour.
1 oz. butter.
3 oz. onion.
2 oz. grated Pfefferkuchen.
Lemon juice.
Salt.

½ teaspoonful Liebig's Meat Extract, dissolved in ¼ pint water.
3 tablespoonsful finely-chopped soup herbs.
1 tablespoonful raspberry syrup.
A pinch of allspice.

Brown the flour with the butter, stir in the broth and beer, then the onion cut into slices, the soup herbs finely chopped, the spice, and lastly, the grated Pfefferkuchen and raspberry syrup. Let the whole simmer for half an hour, then pass through a sieve and flavour with lemon juice, salt and sugar.

In this sauce, carp, Vienna sausages, little meat dumplings, etc., are cooked.

Hollandische Sauce
(Dutch Sauce.)

For 6 Persons.   *Time of Preparation:* 1 hour.

½ pint stock *or* water in which fish or vegetables have been boiled.
3 oz. butter.
½ oz. flour.

5 yolks of eggs.
Juice of 1 lemon.
Salt.
½ teaspoonful Liebig's Meat Extract.

Put the flour with 1 oz. butter in a saucepan and stir until a delicate golden colour. Add the stock and stand on one side to cool. Beat up the yolks of eggs well with the lemon juice, add to them the cooled, thickened stock and the Meat Extract and put into a double milk saucepan. Stir well till the sauce begins to thicken, then add 2 oz. butter and continue stirring until the sauce is quite thick. It must not be allowed to boil.

This sauce may be served with fish, chicken, veal, asparagus, cauliflower, etc., the liquid employed in making it being always the water in which the meat, poultry, fish or vegetables in question have been boiled. It may be modified by the addition of 2 oz. caviar, or ¾ oz. Sardellen or oysters, or ½ tablespoonful dill, or 1 tablespoonful horseradish, or 2 tablespoonsful finely-chopped mushrooms, as circumstances direct.

Mostrich-Sauce
(Mustard Sauce.)

For 6 Persons.   *Time of Preparation:* ¾ hour.

2 tablespoonsful German mustard. | A little vinegar.
½ pint water. | 2 oz. butter.
1 heaped tablespoonful flour. |

Dilute the mustard with the water, bring it to the boil and stir in the butter and then the flour which has been previously smoothly mixed with ½ gill water. Add vinegar, salt, and sugar to taste. Should the sauce be required for haddock, omit the sugar.

Sauce Béarnaise I.

For 6 Persons.   *Time of Preparation:* 1 hour.

8 shallots. | 1 pint Tarragon vinegar.
3 oz. butter. | 1 teaspoonful finely-chopped parsley.
6 pounded peppercorns. | 1 teaspoonful Liebig's Meat Extract.
1 pint Moselle. | 6 yolks of eggs.

Put on the wine, vinegar, shallots and pepper together, and boil till the quantity is reduced by half. Then strain through a cloth and add Meat Extract. When cool pour into an enamel saucepan, add the yolks of eggs, butter, salt, and stir briskly till just before it boils.

This sauce is excellent for fish, poultry, veal cutlets or chops.

Sauce Béarnaise II.

4 yolks of eggs. | 2 tablespoonsful lemon juice.
2 oz. butter. | 2 tablespoonsful broth.
A pinch of pepper. | A pinch of English mustard.

Place all ingredients in a double milk saucepan or in a jug in boiling water and stir continuously till the sauce thickens.

Senfbutter zu Fisch
(Mustard Butter for Fish.)

4 oz. butter. | 1 tablespoonful lemon juice.
4 oz. German mustard (Senf). | 1 tablespoonful chopped parsley.

2 yolks of eggs.	½ teaspoonful Liebig's Meat Extract,
A pinch of English mustard.	dissolved in ½ gill water in which the fish has been boiled.

Brown the butter and add it to all the other ingredients in an enamel saucepan, or, better still, in a double milk saucepan, stirring continuously till the sauce thickens.

Sauce zu Blumenkohl, Spargel, Schwarzwurzeln
(Sauce for Cauliflower, Asparagus or Salsify.)

For 6 Persons.   *Time of Preparation:* ½ hour.

1 pint water in which the vegetables have been boiled.	1 teaspoonful Liebig's Meat Extract, dissolved in the water.
3oz butter,	A pinch of nutmeg.
2oz flour.	

Brown half the butter with the flour to a golden colour, add the vegetable water, stir in the remaining butter, flavour with salt and nutmeg to taste and bring to the boil.

The sauce is improved if half the quantity of vegetable water is omitted and sour or sweet cream taken instead. The cream should then be stirred into the browned flour and butter, before the water be added.

Some prefer to add the yolks of 2 eggs and flavour with lemon juice and sugar.

Finely-chopped parsley may also be added.

Kalte Hering-Sauce
(Cold Herring Sauce.)

For 6 Persons.   Time of Preparation: 1¼ hour.

1 salt herring.	4 hard-boiled yolks.
1 teaspoonful chopped parsley.	A pinch of pepper.
1 teaspoonful chopped onion.	A pinch of English mustard.
1 teaspoonful capers.	4 tablespoonsful salad oil.
3 hard-boiled eggs.	6 tablespoonsful Tarragon vinegar.

Soak the herring in water for 8 hours, then remove the skin and bones and chop finely.

Rub the hard-boiled yolks and stir in the oil and vinegar and then the other ingredients.

Six tablespoonsful of thick cream may be substituted for the oil.

The sauce is also greatly improved if 3 oz. Sardellen are substituted for the herring.

Red Mayonnaise

To make red mayonnaise, pound in a mortar the spawn of a boiled lobster, rub through a fine sieve and add to the mayonnaise, made in the ordinary manner.

Green Mayonnaise

To make green mayonnaise, stir in finely-chopped fresh herbs to the finished mayonnaise.

Cumberland Sauce

For 6 Persons.   *Time of Preparation:* 1 hour.

2 tablespoonsful red wine.	1 tablespoonful orange syrup.
2 tablespoonsful German mustard.	1 tablespoonful lemon syrup.
½ teaspoonful dry English mustard.	½ teaspoonful finely-chopped orange
½ gill brown sauce.	peel (coloured portion only).
2 oz. red currant jelly.	1 oz. raspberry jelly.
4 tablespoonsful salad oil.	

Stir well together the jelly, mustard and oil. Add the brown sauce and continue stirring till all is well mixed. Then add the other ingredients gradually.

This sauce is served with hot and cold ham and with boar's head.

Remouladen Sauce

For 6 Persons.   *Time of Preparation:* 1 hour.

4 hard-boiled yolks of eggs.	1 teaspoonful chopped parsley.
1 raw yolk.	Tarragon vinegar, salt and pepper to
2 oz. German mustard.	taste.
¼ pint salad oil.	1 finely-chopped Sardelle.

Rub the yolks of eggs in a mortar and mix to a smooth paste with the raw yolk. Then stir in the oil and mustard, vinegar to taste, the chopped Sardelle, parsley, pepper, salt and a trifle sugar.

A little chopped onion, also capers, may be added.

Sweet Sauces, to be served hot or cold.

Vanillen- oder Mandel-Sauce
(Vanilla or Almond Sauce.)

For 6 Persons.   *Time of Preparation:* 1 hour.

1 pint milk.	2 oz. sugar.
¼ oz. bitter almonds *or* a stick of vanilla.	½ oz. potato flour.
	A pinch of salt.

Mix the potato flour smoothly in a tablespoonful of the milk. Set all the other ingredients on to boil and, when boiling, stir in the mixed potato flour and bring once more to the boil. Strain and serve.

The sauce is improved if the yolks of 2 eggs are added, but in that case, half the quantity of potato flour must be taken.

A little lemon or orange peel, or a dash of Maraschino likewise improves the sauce.

Frucht-Sauce
(Fruit Sauce.)

For 6 Persons.   *Time of Preparation:* ½ hour.

1 pint water.	Fruit syrup.
Pinch of potato flour.	Sugar to taste.

Stir the potato flour smoothly in cold water and add to ½ pint of boiling water to thicken. Then add fruit syrup to taste and sweeten if necessary.

The sauce is improved if half the quantity water be replaced by white wine.

Rotwein-Sauce
(Red Wine Sauce.)

For 6 Persons.   *Time of Preparation*: ¼ hour.

Lemon or orange peel.	A pinch of potato flour.
½ pint water.	Cinnamon.
2 pints red wine.	Sugar to taste.
2 cloves.	

Boil the spice a few minutes in the water, then strain off. Thicken the water with potato flour, add the wine and sweeten to taste.

Weinschaum-Sauce

For 6 Persons.   *Time of Preparation:* ½ hour.

½ pint white wine.   1 tablespoonful lemon juice.
3 oz. sugar.   4 yolks of eggs.

Put all the ingredients in a double milk saucepan, and whisk briskly until the sauce is thick and frothy. The sauce may be more easily prepared if, instead of 4 yolks, 3 yolks and 2 whites of eggs are taken.

Kirschen-Sauce
(Cherry Sauce.)

Stone the cherries, pound them in a mortar with a few of the kernels, boil for 15 minutes in a little water with some slices of lemon, and rub through a coarse sieve. Then boil up again, add sugar, ground cinnamon and cloves to taste, and stir in a little cornflour, mixed smoothly in cold water, to thicken the sauce well. The addition of a little rum is an improvement.

Wild und Geflügel
(*Game and Poultry.*)

Rehrücken.
(Saddle of Venison.)

For 6 to 8 Persons.   *Time of Preparation:* 2 hours.

1 saddle venison.   ½ pint sour cream.
½lb. butter.   ½ pint stock.
3 oz. bacon.   Tablespoonful salt.
A little flour.

Rub the saddle over with a damp cloth, skin it carefully and lard it with the bacon cut into very thin strips. Put the joint into the baking tin, strew salt over it, pour over hot butter, and roast in a very hot oven, adding the stock gradually, and finally the cream, thickened with a little flour.

When done, which will be in about 30 minutes, remove the meat carefully in one piece from the bone, cut slantingly into slices, and then replace in former position on the bone for serving.

Rehkeule
(Leg of Venison.)

Prepare in the same way as saddle. A leg weighing 4½lbs. takes ¾ hour to roast.

Rehblatt
(Shoulder of Venison.)

Prepare in the same way as saddle. Allow 1½ hour roasting time.

Hirschsteaks mit Burgundersauce
(Venison Cutlets with Burgundy Sauce.)

3 lbs. venison cut from the leg.	2 juniper berries.
2 to 3 tablespoonsful Madeira.	1½ pint Burgundy sauce.
6 oz. butter.	A drop or two of lemon juice.
2 oz. mushrooms.	Salt and pepper.

Cut the meat up into slices, beat it a little, sprinkle with salt and pepper, roll in flour and fry in the butter for lo minutes. Make a Burgundy sauce (*see* recipe), add to it the mushrooms, juniper berries, Madeira and lemon juice, and serve with the venison cutlets.

Ragout von Hirschfleisch
(Venison Ragout.)

2½ lbs. cold roast venison.	1 gill venison gravy.
1½ pint brown Grundsauce.	1 gill red wine.
½ teaspoonful chopped onion.	Lemon juice.
1 teaspoonful chopped raspberry jelly.	Cayenne.

Cut the venison into slices or dice. Boil up all ingredients with the gravy for 10 minutes and then put in the venison to warm through before serving. Salt to taste.

For the red wine may be substituted vinegar, a trifle lemon essence, a pickled cucumber (saure Gurke), and an apple. In either case, capers may be added.

Hasenbraten
(Roast Hare.)

For 8 *Persons.*   *Time of Preparation:* 2½ *hours.*

1 pint water with ½ teaspoonful Liebig's Meat Extract dissolved in it.	1 hare.
	2 oz. bacon.

½ pint cream.

A trifle flour.

2 oz. butter.

Salt.

Draw the hare, chop off the ribs and front legs. Wash it once in lukewarm water and several times in cold water. Then skin very carefully, remove all fat and lard very thoroughly with the bacon cut into strips.

Place the hare in a baking tin, pour the butter, hot, over it and roast, basting continually and adding, alternately, the water with the Meat Extract and the cream thickened with a little flour.

Allow about 45 minutes roasting time for a young hare.

Carve before serving, then place together again in its original shape, pouring over it some of the gravy in which it has been cooked.

Should the hare be somewhat old, lard it and then rub it well with the following mixture: 2 tablespoonsful red wine, 1 tablespoonful lemon juice, 1 tablespoonful salad oil. Leave the hare soaking in this for two days and then roast as above, adding, in addition, this mixture in which it has lain.

Hasen-Salmi
(Salmi of Hare.)

For 8 Persons.   *Time of Preparation:* 2 hours.

1 quart water.

1 roast hare with its gravy.

2 oz. onions.

Carrots.

Turnips.

A little celery.

Lemon peel and juice.

2 oz. browned flour.

½ teaspoonful Meat Extract.

A pinch of cayenne.

A little sugar.

Peppercorns.

2 oz. mushrooms.

A gill red wine.

Roast the hare according to last recipe.

Remove the meat from the bones and cut it up into slices.

Chop up the bones quite small and boil for an hour with onions, carrots, turnips, celery, lemon peel and peppercorns in a quart of water, till the broth is reduced to 1 pint in quantity.

Brown the flour, mix it smoothly with a little cold water and boil it with this hare broth for 10 minutes. Strain through a sieve, stir in half a teaspoonful of Meat Extract, and add it to the gravy in which the hare has been roasted.

Chop up the mushrooms finely (if fresh ones are used, warm them through in a little butter), and add them to the gravy, with the red wine, flavouring with cayenne, lemon juice and a little sugar. Bring to the boil.

The meat of the front legs should then be pounded in a mortar and added to this sauce, which must not be allowed to boil any longer. Place in it the slices of hare and serve. Garnish the dish with little crescents of pastry, baked a delicate brown.

Gebratene Rebhühner
(Roast Partridges.)

For 6 Persons.   *Time of Preparation:* 2 hours.

Salt.	½ pint sour cream.
2 young partridges.	A little flour.
6 oz. butter.	4 oz. bacon.
½ pint stock.	

Pluck, draw and singe the birds, wash in cold water, dry with a cloth and rub over with salt. Tie thin slices of bacon round them and place in the baking tin, in which the butter has first been browned. Roast for about ¾ to 1 hour, basting continually, and adding alternately the stock (for which may be substituted Liebig's Meat Extract dissolved in water), and cream. When done, take out, strain the gravy and serve with them.

The birds may be carved in the kitchen, the pieces being arranged in the centre of the dish and round them a border of macaroni with tomato purée, or little potato dumplings, first boiled and then fried. (See recipe: Kartoffelklösse.)

Rebhahn-Potrafka
(Partridge Potrafka.)

Prepare as Duck Potrafka (*see* recipe), allowing 3 partridges to 6 persons. An excellent dish.

Rebhuhn-Salmi
(Salmi of Partridge.)

For 6 Persons.   *Time of Preparation:* 3½ hours.

4 partridges roasted without cream.	½ teaspoonful Liebig's Meat Extract.
½ pint strong brown "Grund-sauce."	1 oz. chopped onions.
1 gill red wine.	1 oz. German breadcrumbs
1 apple.	(Schwarzbrot).
A little sugar.	Peppercorns,
1 pint water.	Lemon juice.

Roast the partridges according to above recipe, allow them to cool, then remove the meat from the bones and cut up three-quarters of it into small dice. Pound the rest in a mortar.

Chop up the bones and boil them for half an hour in a pint of water, with an apple, onions, a little sugar and peppercorns. Strain through a sieve, stir in the Meat Extract and the breadcrumbs and add to the gravy in which the partridges have been roasted, mixed with the brown sauce, prepared according to recipe on page 55.

Flavour with wine, lemon juice and salt, boil up and stir in first the pounded meat and then the sliced meat. The addition of truffles is a great improvement. Garnish with little crescents of pastry, baked a delicate brown.

Fasan
(Pheasant.)

Prepare in the same manner as partridge, either roasted or as Salmi.

Geschmorte jange Hühner
(Braised Chickens.)

For 6 Persons.   *Time of Preparation: 1½ to 2 hours.*

2 chickens, *or* 1 capon.	A teaspoonful potato flour.
4 oz. butter.	Salt.
Parsley.	

Truss, wash, and dry the chickens. Rub over well, both inside and out, with salt and dredge with flour, placing inside each bird a piece of butter and several sprigs of parsley.

Brown 4 oz. butter in a saucepan, place in it the chickens and baste till brown on all sides. Then braise, adding water from time to time.

When the birds are done, take out, and thicken the gravy with potato flour, which has been mixed smoothly first in a little cold water. Bring to the boil and serve with the chickens. The addition of a gill of sour cream is a great improvement.

Huhn mit pikanter Sauce
(Braised Chicken with Piquant Sauce.)

Braise the chicken according to previous recipe, and cut up.

To make the piquant sauce, add to the gravy 2 tablespoonsful of strong brown "Grundsauce" (*see* recipe), 2 tablespoonsful lemon juice, 2 tablespoonsful red wine, 1 chopped Sardelle, a little sugar and a pinch of pepper and boil up. Then add a teaspoonful of chopped parsley and pour over the fowl.

Paprika-Hahn
(Chicken à la Cayenne.)

Braise the chicken according to recipe, and cut up. In making the gravy, substitute wheaten flour for the potato flour to thicken and boil up with half a teaspoonful of chopped onion and half a teaspoonful of cayenne.

Pour over the chicken and serve with a border of macaroni or rice.

Ragout von Huhn
(Chicken Ragout.)

For 6 Persons.   *Time of Preparation:* 3 hours.

2 chickens, *or* 1 capon.	A few mushrooms.
1 pint strong brown "Grundsauce."	A little lemon juice.
2 to 3 Sardellen.	White wine to flavour.

Braise the chickens (*see* previous recipe) and cut them up.

Add to the gravy the strong brown sauce (*see* recipe, page 55) and the mushrooms. Boil up and flavour with the Sardellen chopped finely, lemon juice, and white wine, and pour over the chicken.

The Same, Richer

Cut up the meat from the breast in slices, and cut off the drumsticks. The remaining meat should be removed from the bones and pounded in a mortar, and added to the sauce, which is flavoured as above. The sliced meat and drumsticks are then served in this sauce.

A further improvement is the addition of calves' sweetbreads and little balls made of veal or fish. (See Kalbfleisch- and Fischklösschen.) 2 oz, caviar or some oysters may be substituted for the Sardellen.

Frikassee iron Huhn
(Chicken Fricassee.)

For 10 Persons.   *Time of Preparation:* 3½ hours.

2 chickens.	Lemon juice.	Cauliflower *or* Aspara-
6 yolks.	An onion.	gus.
2 calves' tongues.	Mushrooms.	A little Madeira.
½ lb. fish, minced.	15 crayfish.	A few peppercorns.
½ lb. sweetbread.	Capers.	Puff paste.
½ lb. pork	2½ pints fricassee	Chopped parsley.
Carrots.	sauce.	3 whole eggs.
2 oz. breadcrumbs.	Sardellen.	2 oz. butter.
Turnips.		

Put on to boil, in 2 quarts water, the chickens, tongues, and sweetbreads with carrots, turnips, onion and a few peppercorns. The sweetbreads not needing so long to cook are taken out first and rinsed at once in cold water.

When the tongue is cooked, skin it and keep it warm in a little of the broth, with the chickens.

Chop up or mince the fish finely and make it into little fish balls with 1 oz. breadcrumbs, 1½ oz. butter and an egg.

Mince the pork and make up also into little balls with an egg,, ½ oz. butter and ½ oz. breadcrumbs. Boil both sets of balls in the chicken broth.

Boil the crayfish in salt water and stuff the heads with the following stuffing: 1 egg, ½ oz. breadcrumbs, ½ oz. butter, some chopped parsley, the chicken livers chopped finely, the meat out of the crayfish claws and salt. Boil the stuffed crayfish heads in the chicken broth.

Cut up the chickens into small portions, the sweetbreads and tongues into slices and arrange on a dish with the meat and fish balls.

Make a fricassee sauce (*see* recipe), using the chicken broth for the purpose, and flavour it with lemon juice, mushrooms, capers, Sardellen and a little Madeira, and stir in the yolks of 6 eggs.

Pour the sauce over the meat.

Garnish with the stuffed crayfish, cauliflower or asparagus, little crescents of puff paste, baked a delicate brown, and parsley.

Reis mit Huhn
(Chicken Rice.)

For 6 Persons.	*Time of Preparation:* 2 hours.

½ lb. rice.	¾ pint fricassee sauce.
2 chickens,	1 tablespoonful salt.
1½ pint water.	Soup herbs (carrots, turnips, parsley
1 onion.	root, celery, etc.).
1 tablespoonful chopped parsley.	A little Meat Extract.

Scald the rice well and fill with it the bottom of a well-buttered pudding mould, that has a tightly-fitting lid to it. Cut each chicken into 6 pieces, sprinkle with the parsley and lay on the rice. Dissolve the butter, boil it up with the water and salt, and pour into the mould. Close the latter and boil for 2 hours.

With the giblets, soup herbs and a little Meat Extract, make ¾ pint stock and with it prepare a fricassee sauce. (*See* recipe.)

Turn out the chicken and rice on to a deep dish and serve with the sauce.

Tomato purée, green peas and cauliflower, or chopped mushrooms may be cooked with the chicken and rice and greatly improve the flavour of the dish.

Perlhuhn
(Guinea Fowl.)

Prepare in the same manner as capon and chicken, also for ragouts and fricassees.

Geschmorte Tauben
(Braised Pigeons.)

For 6 Persons.   *Time of Preparation:* 2 hours.

6 young pigeons.	1 oz. breadcrumbs,
4 oz. butter.	¾ oz. butter.
1 gill cream.	2 eggs.
1 teaspoonful flour.	1 yolk.
1 teaspoonful minced pork.	Nutmeg and salt to taste.

Wash and dry the pigeons well and rub over, inside and out, with salt. Chop up the livers, gizzards and hearts very finely and mix with the eggs, breadcrumbs, parsley and a little nutmeg and salt to taste, to form a stuffing with which the crops are filled.

Braise the pigeons in 4 oz. butter, adding water from time to time, and finally (when the pigeons are done and taken out) a gill of cream, thickened with a teaspoonful of flour, to form a sauce, which should be brought to the boil.

The pigeons may be served with a border of stewed chestnuts, or of rice and green peas, in the latter case the dish is called "Rizi Pizi."

Tauben-Frikassee
(Pigeon Fricassee.)

This is prepared in the same manner as Chicken Fricassee. (*See* recipe.)

Pute Oder Truthahn
(Roast Turkey.)

For 8 Persons.   *Time of Preparation*: 3½ hours.

One turkey.   ¾ lb. butter.

(For the stuffing.)

1 oz. breadcrumbs.	The turkey liver.
4 oz. butter.	2 oz. bacon.
2 eggs.	½ teaspoonful chopped onions.
2 oz. pork fat.	1 oz. fresh truffles. (*or* ¼ oz. dried
4½ oz. boiled lean pork.	truffles.)
2 boiled pigs' kidneys.	Some chopped parsley.
5 oz. cold roast veal.	A pinch of pepper and salt.

Pass the pork fat, lean boiled pork and roast veal twice through the mincing machine. Boil the kidneys, cut them into dice, mix the fat, pork, veal and kidneys with the breadcrumbs, eggs, finely-chopped truffles, onions, salt and pepper to form a stuffing. Fill the crop of the turkey with this and then sew it together.

Rub the turkey inside with salt, chopped parsley and lemon juice, and rub salt over the outside of the turkey also. Place then in a deep baking tin with a pint of boiling water. For 15 to 20 minutes, let the turkey stew in the water alone. Then add ¾ lb. browned butter and roast, basting well, till done.

Truthahn-Frikassee and Ragout
(Turkey Fricassee and Ragout.)

These are prepared in the same manner as Chicken Fricassee and Ragout.

Gänsebraten
(Roast Goose.)

Rub the goose over, inside and out, with salt. Place in it several stalks of marjoram and fill with little apples, then sewing together. The apples should be cored, but not peeled. For only apples may be substituted a mixture of 1 lb. apples, peeled and cut up, ¼ lb. sultanas, and a tablespoonful each of sugar and breadcrumbs; or a mixture of 1 lb. apples, peeled and cut up, and 1 lb. chestnuts, boiled and peeled.

Place the goose breast downwards, in the deep baking pan, pour over it a pint of boiling water, place an onion in the tin, and put into a mediumly hot oven. Let it remain so for half an hour, then turn it. Prick the skin round the wings and legs frequently, to let the fat run out. Baste well and add more water whenever it has boiled away in cooking and the goose is roasting too quickly. The roasting should occupy from 2 to 2½ hours, and the goose should be then of a bright brown colour. At the very last, a few spoonsful of cold water should be poured over the goose, which should then be allowed to continue roasting for a few minutes, that the skin may become crisp.

Remove the fat from the gravy, which may be thickened with a little flour or grated Pfefferkuchen.

Gänseklein
(Goose Giblets.)

Head, neck, gizzard, heart, feet, and the greater part of the wings.	Carrots and turnips.
¼ teaspoonful chopped parsley.	1 quart water.
Peppercorns.	3 oz. flour.
	2 oz. butter.

Clean the giblets, etc., well, cut the wings and neck into small pieces, scald the feet and skin them. Put on in boiling water with carrots and turnips and a little celery and peppercorns and stew until done. Then take out the giblets and strain off the broth.

Prepare a white "Grundsauce" (see recipe, page 55) with the butter, flour, and the broth, which should have boiled down to about 1½ pint. Flavour with finelychopped parsley and pour over the giblets.

Little meat balls, or Semmelor Kartoffelklösse (see recipes, page 22) boiled in the sauce, are an improvement to this dish.

Gänseklein auf polnische Art
(Goose Giblets, Polish Fashion.)

Stew the giblets as directed in previous recipe. With the broth prepare, however, a brown "Grundsauce" (*see* recipe) and boil up in it ½ lb. apples, sliced, flavouring with a little marjoram, sugar and vinegar, and serving with little meat balls of pork (made; with ½ lb. pork, 1 egg and ½ oz. breadcrumbs) or fried sausages.

Gänse-Weisssauer
(Goose in Aspic.)

1 goose, weighing about 9 or 10 lbs.	Some celery.
4 pigs' trotters.	Marjoram.
4 large onions.	One small piece of ginger.
2 slices lemon.	Peppercorns.
Tarragon vinegar.	7 pints water.
2 large parsley roots.	Salt.

Cut the goose up into small pieces. Clean the trotters well and chop them quite small. Put them on to boil in 3½ pints water, skim well, and boil briskly for half an hour. Then add the pieces of goose and the remaining 3½ pints water, and when it has again been well-skimmed, add the onion, celery, parsley, marjoram, peppercorns, salt and vinegar. Boil till all is tender. Then take out the pieces of goose and arrange on a deep dish. Strain off the broth (reduced to about 2 quarts), remove any fat, add more vinegar and salt if necessary clear with white of egg and pounded eggshells, strain through a cloth and pour over the meat. Should gelatine be used instead of pigs' trotters, reckon ½ oz. to each quart of broth.

Gebratene Gans auf mecklenburgische Art
(Roast Goose in Mecklenburg Manner.)

Draw and clean the goose in the usual way and stuff it with the following mixture: Peel and core 8 apples and cut them into quarters. Mix with them 14 oz. sultanas and currants and add a little cinnamon. Mix with 3 handfuls of fine breadcrumbs and 2 beaten-up eggs.

Stuff the goose with this and put it in a baking-pan with ½ pint water. Spread butter over it and bake 2 hours, basting frequently.

While the goose is cooking, shred a medium-sized red cabbage and put it on to simmer in a little stock. When nearly soft, add 6 small sausages, slightly fried in goose fat, and when the cabbage is quite soft, stir in 3 tablespoonsful vinegar.

When the goose has been roasted a nice brown, serve it with the red cabbage and sausages. Add a little broth to the gravy, boil it up and strain it.

Geschmorte Ente
(Braised Duck.)

Brown 2 oz. butter in a deep baking-pan. Place in it the duck, prepared as in the recipe for goose, and baste well. Then add a pint of stock (or water with half a teaspoonful of Liebig's Meat Extract dissolved in it) and some soup herbs, such as carrots, turnips, and a little celery and parsley root, and braise the duck in this, turning frequently, and adding water whenever the gravy seems much reduced in quantity. When the duck is done, take out, and cut up.

Thicken the gravy with a very little flour and pour over the duck, which may be served with various vegetables arranged in little heaps around it.

Geschmorte Ente mit Maronen
(Braised Duck with Chestnuts.)

Braise the duck as in previous recipe. When cooked, add 1 gill red wine, a little lemon peel and 1 lb. stewed chestnuts. When the duck has stewed in this for 5 minutes, take it out and cut it up.

Arrange the pieces in the centre of the dish, the chestnuts in a border around it, outside them baked apples and little roasted potatoes, and pour over the sauce.

Ente-Potrafka
(Polish Duck Ragout.)

For 6 Persons.   *Time of Preparation:* 4 hours.

1 duck.	½ pint sour cream.
2 oz. dried Steinpilze.	3 oz. onions.
½ lb. minced pork.	1 oz. flour.
1 egg.	Peppercorns.
2 oz. butter.	1 teaspoonful Liebig's Meat Extract.
½ oz. breadcrumbs.	Salt.

70

Rub the duck well with salt (inside and out), place a few stalks of marjoram inside it and roast it a nice brown. Cut the giblets up into small pieces and boil with onions, salt and 1 quart water, till the broth is boiled down to about ¾ pint. Then strain off. Wash the Steinpilze and boil for 10 minutes in the broth with a little Meat Extract; then chop finely.

Mince the pork and liver finely and mix with 1 egg, ½ oz. breadcrumbs and a teaspoonful of chopped Steinpilze. Make up into small sausage-shaped rolls, half an inch thick and an inch long, and fry them for 3 minutes in 2 oz. butter.

Place the roasted duck on a board and chop it up into 10 to 12 pieces.

Remove fat from the gravy, add the broth to it, half a pint of sour cream, thickened with 1 oz. flour and the remaining chopped Steinpilze. Boil up once more, put in the little meat rolls and let them warm through in the same for 2 minutes. Pour the sauce first into a mediumly-deep dish, then put the pieces of duck in the centre, round them the little meat rolls, and outside them a border of macaroni and little baked potatoes.

Entenklein. (Duck Giblets.)

Prepare in the same manner as Goose Giblets (see recipe).

Ente in Gelée (Duck in Aspic)

Prepare in the same manner as Goose in Aspic (see recipe).

Entenbraten (Roast Duck.)

Prepare in the same manner as Roast Goose (see recipe).

Rindfleisch
(Beef.)

Rinderbrast gerollt
(Rolled Breast of Beef.)

For 6 Persons.   *Time of Preparation:* 4 hours.

4 lbs. meat.	1 oz. salt.
2 quarts water.	

Take out the bones, roll the meat, tie round with string and boil gently for 3 hours.

Serve with horseradish sauce.

The meat may also be served, cut into slices, on a flat dish with little heaps of various vegetables arranged round it. The vegetables, such as peas, beans, cauliflower and also rice, or macaroni, should have been boiled in broth, either stock or water with Meat Extract dissolved in it. Butter dissolved in some of this vegetable broth should then be poured over the vegetables.

Gedämpftes Rindfleisch
(Stewed Beef.)

For 6 Persons.   *Time of Preparation:* 4 hours.

3 lbs. breast of beef.	2½ pints water.	Soup herbs.

Remove the bones and put them on to boil in 2½ pints water. When they have boiled for an hour, take them out and put into the water the soup herbs, cut up, and the meat, which has meanwhile been well beaten, rolled together and tied up with string.

Simmer for 3 hours. The broth must only just cover the meat.

When the meat is ready, use the broth in preparation of any sauce that may be preferred.

The dish may be garnished with little heaps of various vegetables.

Rindersauerbraten

For 6 Persons.   *Time of Preparation:* 3 hours.

2 to 3 lbs. meat.	½ teaspoonful chopped thyme.
1 tablespoonful German mustard.	3 oz. butter.
1 tablespoonful chopped onions.	A pinch of ground pepper.
1 leaf of sage.	A pinch of salt.

| ½ pint water in which ½ teaspoon-ful Meat Extract is dissolved. | 2 oz. grated Pfefferkuchen *or* 1 oz. flour, to thicken the sauce. |
| | ¼ pint Tarragon vinegar. |

Mix all the ingredients, with the exception of the Pfefferkuchen, to a sauce the consistency of purée. Place the meat in a small earthenware jar, pour the sauce over it and tie down. Stand in a cool place for 3 or 4 days, turning daily.

On the fourth day, braise the meat in a saucepan with 3 oz. butter. The sauce in which it has lain is added gradually and the grated Pfefferkuchen strewn over on serving.

It is an improvement if red wine be taken instead of vinegar.

The meat can also be larded before being placed in the sour mixture.

Binderschmorfleisch

For 6 Persons.   *Time of Preparation:* 3 to 3½ hours.

3 lbs. meat.	Soup herbs.	A piece of dry crust.
1 oz. bacon.	½ oz. salt.	1 oz. flour.
2 oz. onions.	4 oz. butter *or* dripping.	A little spice.

Beat the meat well and tie it together. Cut the bacon into thin strips, sprinkle with pepper and salt, and lard the meat with it.

Rub the meat with the salt and dredge a little flour over it.

Brown the butter or fat in a deep baking-pan, put into it the meat and let it get brown on all sides. Then add the onion, soup herbs, etc., and enough water for the lower half of the meat to be always standing in a thickish gravy.

When the meat is done, take it out, removing the string, and prepare the sauce.

If it is not yet thick enough, add a little flour, then strain through a sieve. A gill of sour cream, or of butter-milk in which a little flour has been smoothly mixed, may be added as an improvement. A further improvement is the addition of 3 tablespoonsful of red wine.

Binderschmorbraten mit Gemüse

For 6 Persons.   *Time of Preparation:* 3½ hours.

2 to 3 lbs. meat.	4 heads of Kohlrabi with the green.
½ lb. spring carrots.	6 oz. cauliflower, *or* asparagus, *or*
1 pickled cucumber.	Brussels sprouts, *or* mushrooms.
½ lb. potatoes.	6 or 8 oz. butter *or* dripping.
2 oz. kidney beans.	

More butter or dripping must be taken than usual, as the vegetables absorb a large amount of it.

The meat is cooked according to previous recipe and the vegetables added gradually, first those that require the longest time to cook. Use whatever vegetables are in season — in winter, those in tins or bottles.

In the last 5 minutes, add the pickled cucumbers, cut into slices. If chopped mushrooms are added, they also must only stew 5 minutes.

The appearance of the dish is improved if some of the vegetables are cooked separately in water with salt.

To serve, cut the meat into slices; place them close together again, lay the vegetables round in little heaps, and pour over the sauce. Then place the vegetables, cooked in water, on the top of the meat and surround all by a border of macaroni. A few stuffed tomatoes among the vegetables improve the appearance of the dish.

The Same, without Soup Herbs.

In the last half-hour add to the gravy the meat is cooking in, 4 oz. mushrooms, 2 teaspoonsful chopped onions, and 1 gill sour cream.

Instead of these, 2 oz. chopped onions and 1 teaspoonful pounded carraway seeds may be substituted, or fresh or pickled cucumbers. The cucumbers must be peeled, the seeds extracted and cut into slices, which are cooked in the gravy for half an hour, with a little sugar, 1 teaspoonful German mustard and a little vinegar.

Rinderroulade
(Beef Olives.)

For 6 Persons.   *Time of Preparation:* 3 hours.

2½ to 3 lbs. meat without bones.	2 oz. finely chopped onions.
4 oz. chopped bacon.	½ oz. salt.
5 oz. breadcrumbs (German bread, if possible).	1 oz. flour.
	A pinch of pepper.
4 oz. butter.	

Cut the meat into slices, about 8 oz. in weight, beat them and sprinkle with salt and pepper

Fry the breadcrumbs with 1 oz. butter, and while still hot, mix with the chopped onion.

Spread the slices of meat with the chopped bacon, and the fried breadcrumbs and onions, and roll together, tieing the ends of the little rolls with string, or skewering them.

Dredge the "Rouladen" with flour, brown the butter, put in the "Rouladen," and brown them on all sides. Then add sufficient water to enable them to stew in a gravy of the same thick consistency as that in which the braised beef is cooked.

Sour cream may be added to the sauce, which may also be flavoured with tomatoes, red wine or Madeira. Sardellen and pickled onions, both chopped finely, may be substituted for the stuffing.

Deutsches Beefsteak
(German Beefsteaks.)

For 6 Persons.　　　　　　*Time of Preparation:* 1 hour

2½ lbs. lean meat.	5 oz. butter.	A pinch of pepper.
1 tablespoonful salt.	1 oz. breadcrumbs.	

Pass the meat through the mincing machine. Mix the breadcrumbs well with an oz. of butter, the salt and pepper, and add to the meat.

Make 12 round rissoles, flattened. Dip a knife in water and trace squares on the rissoles with the back of it.

Fry in the remainder of the butter for 4 minutes, turning 4 times.

Poached eggs may be served on the "beefsteaks," and they may be garnished with Sardellen or pickled cucumbers, cut into slices.

(Prussian Cutlets.)

1½ lb. lean beef, mutton or veal.	A little grated nutmeg.
3 oz. fat.	Salt and pepper to taste.
1 dessertspoonful chopped onion.	

Pass the meat twice through the mincing machine and thoroughly mix in the other ingredients. Divide into portions and press into the shape of cutlets. Insert a little piece of macaroni at the thin end of each to look like a bone. Brush over with egg and sprinkle with breadcrumbs. Fry in hot fat till a nice brown. Place in a circle on a hot dish, with a garnish of vegetables in the centre.

Rindfleischreste mit Aepfeln
(Cold Beef with Apples.)

For 6 Persons.　　　　　　*Time of Preparation:* 1 hour.

1 lb. cold beef.	1¼ lb. pint brown sauce.	1 lb. apples.

Cut the apples into slices and stew in the brown sauce (*see* recipe). Flavour sauce with lemon juice or vinegar and a little sugar and place the slices of cold beef in it just long enough to warm through.

Pickled cucumbers may be substituted for apples.

Restepudding
(Remnant Pudding.)

For 6 Persons.   *Time of Preparation:* 2½ hours.

1 lb. boiled or roast cold meat.
½ lb. bacon.
2 oz. breadcrumbs.
4 tablespoonsful stock.
5 eggs.

2 or 3 Sardellen.
1 teaspoonful chopped parsley.
1 teaspoonful chopped onion.
Pepper and salt to taste.

Pass the meat through the mincing machine, mix thoroughly with all other ingredients, put into a well-buttered pudding basin and boil for 1½ hour.

Serve with Sardellen, Mustard, or Fricassee Sauce.

Rinder- und Kalbszunge
(Ox and Calves' Tongues.)

Cut off the gullet portion, scald and scrape the tongue and boil it in 3½ quarts water, with 1 oz. salt and soup herbs.

Cut the tongue into slices and serve with any of the following sauces: Madeira, Burgundy, Sardelle, Raisin, Mustard or Horseradish. (See the various recipes.)

Rinderzungen-Ragout
(Ox Tongue Ragout.)

For 12 to 14 Persons.   *Time of Preparation:* 4 hours.

1 ox tongue.
1 lb. calves' sweetbreads.
2 ox brains.
1 quart Madeira or Burgundy sauce.

1 lb. pork, made into meat balls with
1 egg and ½ oz. breadcrumbs.
½ lb. bottled button mushrooms.
A little lemon juice.

Boil an ox tongue according to recipe, and then the meat balls and the sweetbreads in the same broth. Boil the brains (*see* recipe) and fry them in butter. With the broth make a Burgundy or Madeira sauce. Cut the tongue and sweetbreads into slices.

Chop up half the quantity of mushrooms, slice the rest. Flavour the sauce with lemon juice and the chopped mushrooms.

Then add all the meat to the sauce, keeping back a few meat balls and the brains to garnish the dish.

The dish may be further garnished with little stewed onions, stuffed tomatoes, or stewed chestnuts. A ring of rice may be placed round the ragout.

Rinderleber geschmort
(Braised Ox Liver.)

For 6 Persons.   *Time of Preparation:* 3 hours.

2½ lbs. liver.	4 oz. butter.
4 oz. bacon.	1 quart milk.
½ pint sour cream.	1 onion.
½ pint water with a teaspoonful Meat	Soup herbs.
Extract dissolved in it.	Salt.
1 oz. flour.	A little spice.

Skin the liver, and soak it in the milk for 1½ hour. Then lard it with strips of the bacon.

Brown the butter, put into it the liver, salt, spice, onion, and soup herbs. Stew gently for 1½ to 2 hours, adding the broth gradually, and finally the cream, thickened with flour.

Pass the sauce through a sieve and pour it over the liver on serving.

Rinderbrägen
(Ox Brains.)

For 4 Persons.   *Time of Preparation:* 1 hour.

Soak an ox brain in water containing vinegar or lemon juice, 1 teaspoonful to half a pint. Then boil for 12 minutes in another lot of water, with lemon juice and salt and place on a sieve to drain.

Cut into four slices, roll in flour, egg and breadcrumbs, and fry in butter.

Garnish with Sardellen, slices of lemon and parsley. Madeira Sauce may be served with the brains.

Ungarisches Goulasch
(Hungarian Goulasch.)

For 6 Persons.   *Time of Preparation:* 3 hours.

3 lbs. beef, without bones.	½ teaspoonful cayenne.
6 oz. bacon, cut into dice.	A pinch of salt.
½ pint cream, in which 1 dessert-	A pinch of pepper.
spoonful flour has been smoothly	½ pint water, in which 1 teaspoonful
mixed.	Liebig's Meat Extract is dissolved.
4 oz. chopped onion.	

Place the meat and bacon, both cut into dice, with the onions, salt and pepper into a saucepan. Pour over them the water, in which the Meat Extract has been dissolved and simmer gently, with the lid of the saucepan on, for 1 hour. Then add the cream and cayenne and continue simmering gently until the meat is quite tender. Should the gravy then be at all thin, it may be thickened by the addition of flour.

Kalbfleisch

(Veal.)

Gekochtes Kalbfleisch mit Frikassee Sauce
(Boiled Veal with Fricassee Sauce.)

For 6 Persons.   *Time of Preparation:* 2 hours.

2 to 3 lbs. veal.	Lemon juice.	3 oz. flour.
1 onion.	3 oz. butter.	2 tablespoonsful salt.
A little spice.	Soup herbs.	
2 yolks of eggs.	1 teaspoonful capers.	

Wash the meat with cold water, cut up into pieces large enough for a helping, put into a saucepan, add the soup herbs, onion and salt, pour boiling water over to nearly cover, and stew till tender. Then strain off the broth.

Brown the butter and flour, and add to the broth to make a sauce. Boil up, add the capers and 2 yolks of eggs and flavour with lemon juice.

Macaroni may be served with this dish, and cauliflower boiled with the veal is an improvement.

Feines Frikassee von Kalbfleisch
(Fricassee of Veal.)

For 6 Persons.   *Time of Preparation:* 2 hours.

1½ lb. knuckle of veal.	½ teaspoonful sugar.
1 lb. tinned asparagus heads.	2½ pints water.
6 yolks of eggs.	3 oz. butter.
A little spice.	2 oz. butter.
1 tablespoonful chopped mushrooms.	1 gill Rhine wine or Moselle.
1 tablespoonful lemon juice.	1 onion.
A little Meat Extract.	1 parsley root.

Boil the onion, parsley root, and spice in the water for half an hour, then add the Meat Extract.

Cut the veal into dice and boil in the broth with salt till tender, but not too soft. Strain off the broth.

Brown the flour and butter and add the broth (which should be nearly a pint) with half the wine, 4 tablespoonsful of water in which the asparagus has been boiled and the chopped mushrooms, and finally the yolks of eggs well beaten with the lemon juice and the remaining wine.

Warm up the meat and asparagus in this sauce and serve.

Geschmortes Kalbfleisch
(Braised Veal.)

For 6 Persons.   *Time of Preparation:* 2 hours.

4½ lbs. veal.	Meat Extract is dis-	1 oz. flour.
¼ lb. butter.	solved.	1 onion.
1 pint water in which 1	Salt.	A little spice.
teaspoonful Liebig's	Soup herbs.	Lemon juice.

Scald the veal and then braise it in a saucepan in the browned butter, with the onion, soup herbs, and spice, adding the broth gradually. When the meat is done, strain off the gravy and thicken with flour. Greatly improved by the addition of chopped mushrooms or half a pint of cream.

Geschmortes Kalbfleisch mit legierter Sauce
(Braised Veal with Egg Sauce.)

For 6 Persons.   Time of Preparation: 1½ hour.

3½ lbs. veal.	3 yolks of eggs.
¼ lb. butter.	Lemon juice.
¾ pint water in which ½ teaspoonful	Salt.
Liebig's Meat Extract is dissolved.	Pepper.
1 teaspoonful chopped onion.	

Brown the butter. Rub over the meat with salt, dust it with flour, and put it with the butter, previously browned, into a deep baking-pan in the oven. After half an hour, add the onion, salt and pepper, and then gradually the broth. When the meat is done, take it out, cut into slices and stand aside to keep warm. Let the gravy boil up, thicken with flour, flavour with lemon juice, stir in the yolks of eggs, and pour over the slices of meat. The sauce may be greatly improved by the addition of chopped Sardellen, mushrooms or caviar.

Serve with a border of macaroni, or little fried potatoes.

Geschmorte Kalbsschnitzel
(Braised Veal Cutlets.)

For 6 Persons.   *Time of Preparation:* 1½ hour.

1½ lb. veal cutlets	4 oz. butter.

| 1 teaspoonful Meat Extract dissolved in ½ pint water. | 1 pint thick Bechamel sauce |

Dust the cutlets with flour, slightly fry on both sides in the butter and then put into a saucepan. Pour the butter over them and braise, adding the broth gradually. Just before serving, add the Bechamel sauce, or merely well thicken with flour and add a little more water. Serve with potatoes, rice and pickled cucumbers. (Salzgurken and Senfgurken.)

Kalbfleisch-Roulade
(Veal Olives.)

These are prepared in the same way as Beef Olives.

Kalbsbraten-Pudding
(Roast Veal Pudding.)

½ lb. cold roast veal (chopped fine).	1 tablespoonful cream.
4 yolks of eggs.	½ lb. fresh pork.
4 whites of eggs.	3 Sardellen (chopped fine).
1 oz. butter.	Salt.
1 oz. breadcrumbs.	Pepper.

Pass the pork twice through the mincing machine and mix well with the finely chopped veal and other ingredients, adding the well-whisked whites of eggs last. Fill a well-buttered mould or basin and boil for 1 hour. Serve with Caper or Sardellen Sauce.

Kalbsbraten-Sülze
(Veal Aspic.)

½ lb. cold roast veal.	½ pint water in which 1 teaspoonful
½ oz. chopped ham.	Liebig's Meat Extract is dissolved.
1 Pfeffergurke (pickled cucumber).	Vinegar.
4 leaves gelatine.	

Peel the cucumber and remove the seeds. Cut it and the meat into dice. Dissolve 4 leaves of gelatine in the broth and flavour with vinegar. Pour over the chopped meat and cucumber.   Pour into a mould. When cold, turn out and serve with Remoulade Sauce. (See recipe.)

Kalbfleisch in Gelée
(Boiled Veal in Jelly.)

| 3 lbs. veal. | A little spice. | ½ oz. gelatine. |
| 2 onions. | 1 parsley root. | 2 whites of eggs. |

2½ pints water.	½ pint Tarragon vinegar.	1 tablespoonful salt.

Cut the meat up into slices or dice, put on in boiling water, with salt, removing any scum, add the onions, vinegar and parsley and boil till quite tender. Then remove the meat, add gelatine to the broth (which should have been boiled down to about half its original quantity) clear with 2 whites of eggs and pour through a sieve over the meat, which has been placed in a deep mould.

When turned out, garnish with sliced pickled cucumbers and hard-boiled eggs and serve with Remouladen Sauce (*see* recipe, page 67) *or* Mayonnaise.

Ueberzogenes Kalbskotellett
(Veal Cutlet with Ragout.)

For 6 Persons.   *Time of Preparation:* 2 hours.

6 veal cutlets.	Capers.
1 calves' brain.	3 Sardellen *or* some chopped mushrooms.
3 oz. butter.	
½ lb. calves' sweetbread.	1 gill white sauce, flavoured with 1
¼ lb. veal cut into dice.	tablespoonful lemon juice and with 4
1 oz. grated Parmesan cheese	yolks of eggs stirred into it.
1 oz. grated roll.	

Boil the sweetbreads and brains and chop them up small. Stir them and all the other ingredients into the sauce, so that the latter forms a thick ragout. Beat the cutlets, dust them over with flour and fry them slightly on both sides in 3 oz. butter for 2 minutes. Then lay them on a flat, fireproof dish, and spread a tablespoonful of the ragout on each cutlet. Sprinkle each with Parmesan cheese and breadcrumbs and pour over them the frying butter. Place the dish on a pan of cold water in a hot oven and bake for about 5 minutes.

Kalbsleber
(Calves' Liver.)

For 6 Persons.   *Time of Preparation:* 1 hour.

2 lbs. calves' liver.	½ teaspoonful chopped onion.
4 oz. butter.	1 gill strong broth.
1 gill cream, thickened with a little flour.	A pinch of pepper.
	A pinch of salt.
2 oz. bacon.	

Skin the liver, lard it with the bacon, rub it over with the pepper, salt and onion, and bake it in the oven in a deep pan for 30 minutes in the butter, which must be browned first, adding gradually the broth and cream. Cut into slices and serve with a border of macaroni and cauliflower. Sprinkle thickly with Parmesan cheese and pour over it the sauce in which it has been stewed. The liver may also be cut into slices and simply fried in egg and breadcrumbs.

Kalbsleber-Goulasch
(Calves' Liver Goulasch.)

For 6 Persons.   *Time of Preparation:* ¾ hour.

1½ lb. calves' liver.	½ tablespoonful salt.
1 oz. chopped onion.	1 dessertspoonful flour.
4 oz. butter.	Pinch of pepper.

Skin the liver and cut into small dice. Roll well in flour, pepper and salt.

Brown the butter and throw in the onions and liver and fry for 2 minutes, shaking to and fro continually.

Serve on a very hot dish with a border of rice or macaroni, or of little roast potatoes. Hand round with pickled cucumbers (Senfgurken).

Kalbsleber-Klösse
(Calves' Liver Dumplings.)

For 6 Persons.   *Time of Preparation:* 1¼ hour.

1 lb. calves' liver.	2 eggs.	2 rubbed sage leaves.
1 oz. breadcrumbs.	2 extra yolks.	1 teaspoonful rubbed
4 oz. flour.	1 oz. butter.	marjoram.
3 oz. bacon.	1 oz. bread cut into	
2 tablespoonsful salt	dice.	

Skin the liver, pass through the mincing machine,, then mix well together with the eggs, extra yolks, salt, pepper, marjoram and sage.

Cut the bread into dice and fry in the butter and stir into the mixture.

Form into little dumplings, throw into boiling water and boil for 10 minutes. Then sprinkle breadcrumbs over them and pour over the browned butter.

Serve with Sauerkohl, Schmorkohl, Schmorgurken, potato dishes prepared with vinegar, and lettuce salad.

Should the mixture be too firm, add a little milk, if not firm enough, a little more flour.

Kalbsleber-Brot (Pain)
(Calves' Liver Paté).

Time of Preparation: 2 hours.

1½ lb. calves' liver,	½ teaspoonful chopped onion.
¾ lb. pork fat.	½ teaspoonful rubbed marjoram.
6 oz. fat bacon.	A pinch of pepper.
4 eggs.	1 tablespoonful salt.

Pass the liver and fat several times through the mincing machine, stir in the eggs, then pass through a sieve and add salt and herbs, (The addition of some chopped truffles is a great improvement.) Line a round mould with the bacon cut into very thin slices, fill up with the meat, place a few slices of bacon on the top, and bake in the oven for an hour, standing the mould in a pan of water.

Serve with a piquant sauce. If served cold, garnish with aspic.

Gekochte Kalbsmilch
(Boiled Calves' Sweetbread.)

These are soaked and boiled in water for 40 minutes with salt, and served with various sauces, such as Madeira, Mushroom, Sardellen or Crayfish.

For 6 persons reckon 1½ lb. sweetbreads and ¾ pint sauce.

Geschmorte Kalbsmilch
(Braised Calves' Sweetbread.)

For 6 Persons.   *Time of Preparation:* 1 hour.

1½ lb. sweetbread.	½ tablespoonful salt.
1 tablespoonful lemon juice.	1 teaspoonful flour.
1 gill stock.	2 oz. butter.

Soak the sweetbreads and boil, in boiling water, for 10 minutes. Cut into slices about half an inch thick and roll in flour.

Brown the butter in a saucepan and put in the slices of sweetbread. Add the stock, stew gently for 15 minutes, and flavour the sauce with lemon juice. The sauce may also be improved by the addition of cream, or Sardellen and mushrooms.

Kalbsmilch-Pudding
(Sweetbread Pudding.)

For 6 Persons.   *Time of Preparation:* 3 hours.

1 lb. sweetbread.	6 eggs.
6 oz. rice.	1 quart broth.

Soup herbs.	4 oz. butter.
2 tablespoonsful salt.	A pinch of pepper.
1 tablespoonsful chopped parsley.	A pinch of cayenne.

Soak the sweetbread and boil it with the soup herbs in the broth for 15 minutes. Then take it out, strain off the broth and boil the rice gently for an hour in the latter. Ten minutes before it is finished, add 2 oz. butter. Stand the rice on one side to get cool.

Cream the other 2 oz. butter, add the yolks, parsley and pepper, and, alternately, the rice and whipped white of egg, and finally, the sweetbread cut into small dice.

Fill a well-buttered mould three-quarters full and boil for 1½ hour.

Serve with Sardellen, Crayfish or Caper Sauce. (See Section: Sauces.) May also be garnished with various vegetables, such as cauliflower, green peas, carrots, asparagus or Brussels sprouts.

Kalbsmilch-Croqaettes
(Sweetbread Croquettes.)

To make 12 *Croquettes.*   *Time of Preparation:* 2 hours.

¾ lb. sweetbread.	6 oz. calves' tongue or cold roast veal.
1 leaf of gelatine.	1 gill broth.
1 oz. butter.	2 teaspoonsful lemon juice.
1 oz. flour.	2 yolks of eggs.
8 bottled mushrooms.	Salt.
2 teaspoonsful Madeira.	

Boil the sweetbreads and tongue and cut into small dice with the mushrooms. Make a white sauce of the broth, butter and flour, boil it down to half its original quantity and flavour with lemon juice and salt. Dissolve the gelatine and add to the sauce, with the Madeira and yolks of eggs. Then add the other ingredients and mix to a paste. Spread over a dish on which breadcrumbs have been scattered and put a layer of breadcrumbs on the top. Stand in a cool place for an hour.

Make up into 12 croquettes, roll in flour, egg and breadcrumbs, and fry in butter or dripping. Wash some parsley, dry it with a cloth, fry for half a minute and garnish with it.

Serve the croquettes in a serviette.

Kalbsbrägen
(Calves' Brain.)

For 4 *Persons.*   *Time of Preparation:* 1 hour.

Soak the brain first and then boil gently for 15 minutes in 1 pint water with salt, a teaspoonful of vinegar, onions and a little spice.

Drain on a sieve, cut lengthwise into 4 pieces, roll in flour, egg and bread-crumbs, and fry in 2 oz. butter. The dish may be garnished with Sardellen, and Sardellen or Mushroom Sauce may be served with it. If served cold, then substitute Mayonnaise or Remouladen Sauce.

Ragout fin in Muscheln
(Ragout fin in Scallops.)

Quantity for 12 *Scallop Shells.*

2 calves' brains.	2 oz. butter.
1 tongue.	1 pint thick white sauce.
½ lb. calves' sweetbread	3 Sardellen.
8 yolks of eggs.	2 to 3 tablespoonsful white wine.
10 button mushrooms.	1 oz. grated Parmesan cheese.
Lemon juice to taste	1 teaspoonful capers.

Boil the brains, tongue and sweetbread. Then cut the tongue into narrow strips, the sweetbread into dice, and divide the brains into small pieces with a spoon. Make a pint of thick white sauce, flavour with wine, lemon juice, chopped mushrooms, Sardellen and capers. and stir in the yolks of eggs. Pour the sauce over the meat.

Butter the shells, strew breadcrumbs in them, then fill up with the ragout, putting on top of each shell another sprinkling of breadcrumbs and Parmesan cheese.

Bake in a hot oven for a few minutes.

Kalbszunge mit höllandischer Sauce
(Calves' Tongue with Dutch Sauce.)

For 6 Persons.   *Time of Preparation:* 2½ hours.

Boil 3 small calves' tongues in 1 quart water and then skin them. When cool, cut them into slices lengthwise, roll in egg and breadcrumbs and fry them in 2 oz. butter.

Use the water they have been boiled in to prepare a Dutch sauce (*see* recipe). Pour over the slices and serve.

This dish is improved by the addition of little meat balls (*see* recipes) or button mushrooms.

Kalbfleischring
(Border of Minced Veal.)

½ lb. veal.	¼ lb. pork.	2 tablespoonsful flour.
2 oz. butter.	3 eggs.	A pinch of pepper.
5 mushrooms.	1 gill milk.	

85

Heat half the quantity of the butter, the flour and the milk, in a saucepan, stirring continuously till of the consistency of dough. Then turn into a basin, stir till cold and beat well with the remainder of the butter and the yolks of the eggs. Add salt, pepper, the mushrooms chopped finely and the whites of eggs, whisked well, and finally the veal and pork which have been passed several times through the mincing machine. Stir well and when thoroughly mixed, fill a ring-shaped mould and steam carefully for ½ to ¾ hour. Turn out the ring on to a flat dish and fill the centre with asparagus, cauliflower, peas, Brussels sprouts, meat or fish ragout, rice and green peas, etc.

Hammelfleisch
(*Mutton.*)

Hammelkeule wie Wild
(Leg of Mutton as Mock Venison.)

Bone the mutton, beat it well and lard it with strips of bacon. Place it in sour milk for 3 days and then roast it (2½ hours to a 9 lb. leg) with 2 lbs. butter, pouring in water from time to time. When the meat is done, add to the gravy half a pint of sour cream, thickened with a little flour, and ½ teaspoonful Liebig's Meat Extract.

Hammelkeule mit Mostrich
(Leg of Mutton with Mustard Sauce.)

¼ lb. German mustard.	A pinch of pepper.
1 oz. chopped onion.	1 gill broth made by dissolving ½
2 tablespoonsful salad oil.	teaspoonful Liebig's Meat Extract in
1 tablespoonful chopped parsley.	water.
1 tablespoonful lemon juice.	½ lb. butter.
2 rubbed sage leaves.	1 tablespoonful Tarragon vinegar.

Bone, beat and lard the mutton and then place it from 24 to 48 hours in a sauce composed of the above ingredients.

Then roast in a deep pan in the oven with ½ lb. butter, adding gradually the sauce in which it has lain.

The sauce may be thickened before serving with a little flour, and improved by the addition of a little red wine.

Hammelfleisch-Pudding
(Mutton Pudding.)

For 6 Persons.   *Time of Preparation:* 3½ hours

1¼ lb. lean mutton.	½ lb. bacon.

6 eggs.	1 tablespoonful chopped parsley.
2 oz. breadcrumbs.	1 tablespoonful German mustard.
6 Sardellen.	2 tablespoonsful salt.
1 tablespoonful capers.	

Pass the mutton and bacon twice through the mincing machine. Soak the breadcrumbs in milk and stir to the consistency of purée. Then add the eggs, salt, finely chopped Sardellen, capers, parsley and mustard. Lastly, stir in the meat and mix all well together.

Fill a well-buttered mould or basin and boil for 2 hours. Before the pudding is turned out, run a skewer through a few times.

Serve with Caper, Onion or Sardellen Sauce.

Hammelzungen in Aspic
(Sheeps' Tongues in Aspic.)

For 6 Persons.   *Time of Preparation:* 3 hours.

6 sheeps' tongues.	Soup herbs.	Spice.
½ teaspoonful Liebig's Meat Extract.	½ oz. gelatine.	2 whites of eggs.
	1 quart water.	2 tablespoonsful salt.
1 onion.	1 gill Tarragon vinegar.	

Scald the tongues and scrape them. Put them on to boil with 1 quart water, onions, soup herbs, spice and salt, and boil till very tender. Then remove the hard skin and cut in half lengthwise.

Skim the fat off the broth, which should be reduced to about 1 pint, and add the Meat Extract, gelatine and Tarragon vinegar.

Clear with 2 whites of eggs, strain through a cloth and pour over the sheeps' tongues, placed in glass dishes.

Schweinefleisch
(Pork.)

Gekochtes saures Schweinefleisch
(Boiled Pork.)

For 8 Persons.   *Time of Preparation:* 2 hours.

4½ lbs. pork.	A few peppercorns.
1 lb. onions.	½ teaspoonful Liebig's Meat Extract.
½ lb. apples.	1 oz. rice.
2½ pints water.	4 tablespoonsful vinegar.
1 tablespoonful salt.	

Cut the meat into eight slices and put on in boiling water with the onions, apples, peppercorns, salt and rice. When it has boiled for an hour, add the vinegar. The meat must be boiled till very tender and then taken out and the gravy, to which a little Meat Extract is added, strained through a sieve and poured over it. Pears may be substituted for apples; in this case, after the gravy has been strained off, replace the pears in it.

Schweineohren mit Senfsauce
(Pigs' Ears with Mustard Sauce.)

For 6 Persons. *Time of Preparation:* 3 hours.

3 large pigs' ears.	1 teaspoonful sugar.	½ tablespoonful
2 oz. butter.	A little rubbed marjo-	chopped onion.
2 oz. flour.	ram.	3 tablespoonsful vine-
1 apple.	A few peppercorns.	gar.
½ teaspoonful Liebig's	3 hard-boiled eggs.	1 tablespoonful salt.
Meat Extract.	4 oz. German mustard.	2½ pints water.

Wash the pigs' ears well, cut them in two lengthwise and boil them, till very tender, in 1 quart water with the marjoram, a whole onion, an apple, peppercorns, and salt. Then take out, allow to cool, and cut up into narrow strips.

Strain the broth, brown the butter and flour together and add to it with the chopped onion to make a thick sauce, adding the mustard, sugar, Meat Extract (dissolved in half a pint of water), and the vinegar.

Boil up the pieces of ear once more in the sauce and serve, garnished with hard-boiled eggs.

The ears may also be merely boiled in water with salt, then when cold, cut into strips, rolled in flour, egg and breadcrumbs, fried in butter and served with Remouladen Sauce (*see* recipe).

Gedämpftes Schweinefleisch
(Stewed Pork.)

For 6 Persons. *Time of Preparation:* 2½ hours.

3 lbs. lean pork.	1 quart water.	Lemon juice.
1 oz. flour.	1 tablespoonful German	Soup herbs.
1 onion.	mustard.	

Put on the meat, which should be well hung, in boiling water, with salt, soup herbs, onion and mustard, and boil till tender. There must only be suffi-cient water in the saucepan to just cover the meat the whole time. When done, remove the meat, thicken the gravy with flour, strain, and skim off the fat.

Serve with little dumplings (Mehlklösse), *see* recipe.

The sauce is much improved if, during the last hour of boiling, tomatoes are added, cut in slices and the seeds removed. The sauce must then be rubbed through a sieve and flavoured with sugar and a pinch of cayenne. In this case, the meat is cut in slices, arranged in the centre of the dish, the sauce poured over it, and surrounded by a border of rice, Nudeln, or macaroni.

Schweineschmorbraten
(Braised Pork.)

For 6 *Persons.*   *Time of Preparation:* 2 hours.

3½ lbs. pork.	1 dessertspoonful flour.	½ teaspoonful Liebig's
1 onion.	1 pint water, wine, or	Meat Extract.
1 tablespoonful salt.	Weissbier.	

Wash and beat the meat well, scald with boiling water, dry with a cloth and rub over with salt.

Place in a saucepan with ¼ pint boiling water, and boil briskly till the water has boiled away and the meat browns. *Or,* the meat may be dredged with flour and browned well in a frying pan with 2 oz. butter.

Then place the meat with water, wine, or Weissbier in a saucepan, add onion and soup herbs, and braise. When done, take out and thicken the gravy with flour. Strain through a sieve, remove fat, add a pinch of cayenne and a gill of cream, and stir in half a teaspoonful of Meat Extract.

Tomatoes may also be added to the sauce, as in the last recipe, or half a pound of apples, in which case the cream and cayenne are omitted.

Schweinefleisch als Wild
(Pork as Mock Venison.)

For 8 *Persons.*   *Time of Preparation:* 3 hours.

4½ lbs. pork.	3 juniper berries.	1 teaspoonful flour.
½ pint sour cream.	2 oz. butter.	1 pint stock.

Remove most of the fat from the meat, beat it well and lay it in milk for 4 days. Then take it out and rub it over with salt.

Brown the butter in a deep baking-tin and lay the meat in it. Baste well and roast in the oven, adding the stock from time to time. (Half a pint of water with Meat Extract dissolved in it may be substituted for stock.)

In the last half-hour of roasting add the cream, in which the flour and pounded juniper berries have been well stirred. A great improvement is the addition of chopped mushrooms.

Pikante Schweinekenle
(Piquant Leg of Pork.)

For 15 *Persons.*   *Time of Preparation:* 4 hours.

Leg of pork weighing about 11 lbs.
1 finely chopped Sardelle.
2 leaves of sage.
4 cloves.
1 gill red wine.
2½ pints water with 1 teaspoonful Liebig's Meat Extract dissolved in it.
2 tablespoonsful finely chopped onion.

2 tablespoonsful salad oil.
3 tablespoonsful lemon juice or vinegar.
2 tablespoonsful German mustard.
1 teaspoonful rubbed thyme.
1 tablespoonful marjoram.
1 tablespoonful red currant jelly.
1 tablespoonful flour.

Beat the leg of pork well, remove the crackling and some of the fat and bone it.

Mix the marjoram, thyme, cloves, sage, currant jelly, oil, wine, mustard, lemon juice or vinegar, and onions thoroughly to the consistency of purée and rub well into the meat. Then place latter in an earthenware vessel which it must nearly fill. Boil up the water with salt, add Meat Extract and pour over the meat, which must remain in soak 24 to 48 hours in a cool place.

Then roast the joint, adding from time to time the liquid in which it has lain. Before serving, thicken the gravy with flour and improve, if desired, with cream.

Schweins-Carré mit Kirschen-Sauce
(Chine of Pork with Cherry Sauce.)

Bone a chine of pork, remove superfluous fat and roast with the trimmings, sliced carrots and onions, salt and pepper. Baste frequently and bake slowly, adding stock or water occasionally, to prevent the meat browning.

When almost cooked, place on a deep dish and sprinkle over very thickly with breadcrumbs (in preference, German bread) mixed with a little cinnamon and castor sugar. Replace in a moderate oven and bake for another 20 minutes till the crust is a light brown.

Serve with a thick cherry sauce (*see* recipe).

Schinken in Burgunder
(Ham in Burgundy.)

For 12 *Persons.*   *Time of Preparation:* 5 hours.

1 smoked ham weighing 9 lbs.
1 lb. small onions.
1 oz. sugar.

1 tablespoonful Madeira.
1¼ pint Burgundy.
A pinch of pepper.

1 tablespoonful currant jelly.

2 teaspoonsful Liebig's Meat Extract.

1¼ pint brown sauce.

3 oz. butter.

A drop or two of lemon juice.

Bone the ham and string it together. Boil slowly for from 4 to 5 hours.

Meanwhile scald the onions six times. Brown the butter and sugar, add half a pint of the water in which the ham has been boiled, a drop or two of lemon juice and a teaspoonful of Meat Extract, and stew the onions in it till brown, the sauce being just sufficient to cover them.

When the ham is done, remove the thick skin and lay the ham in a baking-pan. Pour over it some of the brown sauce (in the making of which, water in which the ham has been boiled and Meat Extract are employed) and some of the wine and place in a very hot oven. Add the remaining sauce and wine gradually and baste the ham with it frequently so that it receives a brown glazing. Finally, stir the red currant jelly into the sauce in which the onions were stewed, flavour with cayenne and add to the Burgundy sauce.

Place the ham on a dish, cut into slices and arrange round it different vegetables and chestnuts, macaroni, Sauerkohl and the little stewed onions.

Schinkenscheiben in Burgander-Sauce
(Ham in Burgundy Sauce.)

For 6 Persons.   *Time of Preparation:* 1 hour.

2 lbs. boiled ham.

1 pint Burgundy sauce.

1 lb. little onions, prepared according to previous recipe.

A similar dish to the preceding can be prepared more simply in the following way: —

Prepare a Burgundy sauce with onions according to recipe.

Cut the meat into slices and lay it in the boiling Burgundy sauce, which must not be salted until after the ham is added.

Serve with various vegetables round, as in last recipe.

Bratklops

For 6 Persons.   *Time of Preparation*: 1 hour.

¾ lb. pork.

¾ lb. beef.

½ teaspoonful onions slightly fried in butter.

1½ oz. breadcrumbs.

2 eggs.

½ teaspoonful pounded carraway seeds.

3 oz. butter.

A leaf of rubbed sage.

Salt and pepper.

Mix well together the breadcrumbs, eggs, salt, pepper and carraway, and add to them gradually the meat which has been passed twice through the mincing machine. Form into 14 rissoles and fry in 3 oz. browned butter.

Bratklops to be eaten Cold

For 6 Persons.   *Time of Preparation:* 1 hour.

1½ lb. pork.	Yolks of 2 eggs.
1 oz. breadcrumbs.	White of 1 egg.
4 Sardellen, chopped fine.	½ teaspoonful chopped onions slight-
4 oz. butter.	ly fried in butter.
6 hard-boiled eggs.	Salt and pepper.

Mix the breadcrumbs with the 2 yolks, the white of egg, onions, salt, pepper and chopped Sardellen, and when thoroughly mixed, add the meat, previously passed twice through the mincing machine. Cut each of the hardboiled eggs in two, press the mixture firmly round each piece and fry for 5 minutes a nice brown in 4 oz. butter. Serve cold.

Konigsberger Klops

For 6 Persons.   *Time of Preparation:* 11 hour.

¾ lb. pork.	½ oz. butter.	Salt and pepper.
¼ lb. veal.	1 oz. breadcrumbs.	1 tablespoonful
¾ lb. beef.	3 eggs.	chopped parsley.
½ teaspoonful chopped	1 quart brown sauce.	
onions slightly fried in	1 teaspoonful capers.	
butter.	Lemon juice.	

Mix the breadcrumbs with 1 egg and the butter, and stir in a saucepan till the mixture is reduced to the consistency of dough. Put this into a basin, and stir till cool, adding then the salt, pepper, the remaining eggs and, lastly, the meat which has been passed twice through the mincing machine. Form into 12 long-shaped rissoles, fry them slightly in 2 oz. butter, and then place them to stew gently for 12 minutes in a quart of strong, boiling brown sauce (*see* recipe, page 55).

Flavour the sauce with a teaspoonful of capers, half a teaspoonful chopped onions, slightly fried in butter, and lastly 3 Sardellen, finely chopped, and a tablespoonful of chopped parsley.

The butter in which the Klops have been fried can be rinsed out of the pan with some of the brown sauce, and added to the finished sauce.

The sauce may be varied by the addition of tomato purée, red wine, or Madeira, and is greatly improved by the addition of a gill of sour cream and some dried Steinpilze, which may be obtained at most of the German Delikatessen-Handlungen.

Falscher Hase
(Mock Hare.)

1 lb. pork.	Pepper.	½ teaspoonful capers
½ lb. veal.	1 tablespoonful	1 teaspoonful flour.
4 oz. butter.	chopped onion.	1 teaspoonful English
2 Sardellen.	½ lb. beef.	mustard.
1 gill sour cream *or*	2 oz. butter.	Salt.
milk.	1 oz. breadcrumbs.	
4 eggs.	1 pint broth.	

Pass the meat three times through the mincing machine. Mix the bread-crumbs with 1 egg and the butter and stir in a saucepan till the mixture is reduced to the consistency of dough. Put this in a basin and stir till cool, adding then the 2 eggs and 1 extra yolk and the chopped Sardellen, capers, mustard, onion, salt, and pepper. Lastly, add the meat and the bacon cut into small dice and mix thoroughly. Form into two "loaves," brush over with the remaining white of egg, sprinkle over with grated roll crust, place in browned butter in a deep baking-tin and bake for ¾ hour, adding cream and broth gradually.

The veal may be omitted, or even pork alone taken. If intended for eating cold, it is better to take only pork and spice well with carraway.

The gravy may be improved by the addition of 4 tablespoonsful of red wine and half a pint of brown sauce (*see* recipe).

Gedämpfte Kotelettes
(Pork Chops — Stewed.)

6 pork chops.	2 oz. butter	Pepper.
1 gill white wine.	1 tablespoonful	Salt.
1 gill broth.	chopped onion.	A little flour.

Remove all fat from the chops, rub over with salt and pepper, partly fry on both sides in a deep pan and then add the wine and broth and stew slowly till done. (A teaspoonful of Liebig's Meat Extract dissolved in water may be substituted for broth.)

Thicken the sauce with flour. It may also be thickened with German mustard or the yolks of eggs may be stirred in.

Gefüllter Hackbraten
(Stuffed Mock Hare.)

Ingredients and preparation as for Mock Hare.

When well mixed and formed into a "loaf," place on a pasteboard strewn with grated roll and flatten out. Now place in the middle pieces of hard-boiled eggs and around them, pickled cucumbers cut into thin strips, Sardellen, capers and scraps of ham. Roll together and bake.

Specially good for cutting into slices and eating cold.

Kotelettes in Gelée
(Pork Chops in Aspic).

For 6 Persons.   *Time of Preparation:* 2 hours.

6 chops.	Onions.
10 leaves of gelatine.	Soup herbs.
Peppercorns.	1 gill Tarragon vinegar.
A tablespoonful of salt.	½ teaspoonful Liebig's Meat Extract.
2½ pints water.	

Put the chops on, in boiling water, removing any scum, and then add the soup herbs, onions, peppercorns, salt and vinegar, and boil till tender.

Skim off the fat from the broth, strain, and, if necessary, clear with an egg. Dissolve in it 10 leaves of gelatine and stir in half a teaspoonful of Liebig's Meat Extract.

Pour into a deep dish sufficient to cover the bottom. As soon as it has set, decorate with slices of boiled eggs, pickled cucumbers, Sardellen, etc., and then place in the chops and pour over the rest of the broth.

When cold, cut out the chops separately and serve with Remouladen Sauce (*see* recipe).

Schweinefleisch-Sülze
(Pork in Jelly.)

For 6 Persons.   *Time of Preparation:* 3 hours.

2 lbs. pigs' trotters.	2 quarts water.	A little sugar.
1 lb. lean fresh pork.	3 onions.	1 bayleaf.
½ lb. veal.	1 quart vinegar.	1 clove.
½ lb. lean pickled pork.	Peppercorns.	

Put all the meat on to boil with the onions and peppercorns, and boil till very tender. Then take out, cut into little dice and put into a mould. Add vinegar and sugar to the broth and boil down to a little over a pint. Skim off fat, then strain and pour over the meat in the mould. Sardellen and pickled cucumbers (Pfeffergurken) cut up small may be added to the meat if desired.

Turn out when set.

Gemüse
(Vegetables.)

Stangenspargel
(Asparagus prepared whole.)

Wash the asparagus and peel it. Tie about 8 thick or 12 thinner heads together, trimming off the lower ends of the stalks to an equal length. Place upright in a double enamel saucepan, in boiling water, slightly-salted and sweetened, with sufficient water to just cover the tips. Boil for about half an hour, then take out, place on a warm dish, untie, pour oiled butter over and serve.

The water the asparagus has been boiled in, as well as the peelings (well washed) and the odd ends cut off, should be used for soup.

Bruchspargel

For 6 Persons.   *Time of Preparation:* 1 to 1½ hour.

3½ lbs. asparagus.	1 gill cream.	A tablespoonful salt.
3 oz. butter.	2½ pints water.	A little nutmeg.
2 oz. flour.	A little sugar.	

Wash and peel the asparagus and break it into pieces about 2 to 3 inches long. Boil till tender in 2½ pints water, slightly salted and sweetened. Then drain on a sieve. Put 3 oz. butter into a saucepan and mix 2 oz. flour smoothly with it. Add the cream and a pint of the asparagus water. Boil well and flavour with a little nutmeg. Serve the asparagus in this sauce. The cream may be omitted and extra asparagus water substituted for it; in this case, 1½ oz. fresh butter is added to the sauce and a little chopped parsley stirred in just before serving.

Spargel mit Sauce gebacken
(Asparagus baked in Sauce.)

For 6 Persons.   *Time of Preparation:* 2 hours.

Prepare the asparagus and sauce as in last recipe and fill a mould. Melt an oz. of butter, pour it over, place a layer of Parmesan cheese (2 tablespoonsful) on the top and bake in a very hot oven for 15 minutes, standing the mould in a pan of hot water.

Tinned asparagus may be used equally well for this and other asparagus dishes. When the tin has been opened, stand it in boiling water, till the asparagus is warm through. To make a sauce, some of the water out of the tin may be used.

Spargel in Aspic
(Asparagus in Aspic.)

For 6 Persons.　　　　　　*Time of Preparation:* 2 hours.

2 lbs. fresh asparagus *or* 1 lb. tinned asparagus.	1 tablespoonful salt.
	1 tablespoonful sugar.
¾ pint asparagus water.	½ oz. gelatine.
1 gill Tarragon vinegar.	2 tablespoonsful chopped parsley.
½ teaspoonful English mustard.	A little Liebig's Meat Extract.

Peel the asparagus, cut it into pieces about 2 inches long and boil till tender in 1¼ pint water, with salt and sugar. Take out and place on a sieve to drain. Dissolve the gelatine in ¾ pint of the asparagus water, stir in the Tarragon vinegar, mustard and a little Meat Extract and place on ice. When the aspic begins to set, stir in the chopped parsley and remove from the ice.

Brush over a mould with oil, place on ice, pour in some of the half-set aspic, let it stand till quite set, place a layer of asparagus on it, then again pour in aspic and proceed with alternate layers of aspic and asparagus till the mould is full, the topmost layer being aspic.

Turn the asparagus aspic out on to a glass dish and serve with a Remouladen sauce (*see* recipe), with cold tongue, ham, etc.

Blumenkohl gekocht
(Boiled Cauliflower.)

Remove the leaves from the cauliflower, cut off all stalk and soak the whole heads for a time in water with a little vinegar, so that any insects in the head may come out into the water.

Boil in water only slightly salted, with a little sugar added. When soft, drain on a sieve and serve with browned butter, or with Dutch sauce (*see* recipe) poured over.

An excellent dish is cauliflower or asparagus with a sauce poured over it, served in the centre of a ring of minced veal.

Blumenkohl in Aspic
(Cauliflower in Aspic.)

Prepare in the same way as Asparagus in Aspic (see recipe, previous page), allowing slightly more cauliflower than the quantity of asparagus given.

Blumenkohl mit Uberzug gebacken
(Cauliflower Fritters.)

For 6 Persons.   *Time of Preparation:* 2 hours.

2 lbs. cauliflower.	½ lb. flour.	1 tablespoonful salad
3 pints water.	3 whites of eggs.	oil.
1 gill white wine.		1 teaspoonful salt.

Wash the cauliflower well and break it up into little heads. Boil these and lay them on a sieve to drain and dry.

With the wine, whites of eggs, oil, flour and salt make a thick batter. Dip each little head of cauliflower into the batter and fry a golden brown in a saucepanful of butter.

Cauliflower so prepared is excellent served with Fillet of Beef or Veal with Remouladen Sauce (*see* recipe).

Blumenkohl gebacken
(Baked Cauliflower.)

For 6 Persons.   *Time of Preparation:* 2 hours.

1½ lb. cauliflower.	½ teaspoonful Liebig's	1 gill cream.
2 oz. butter.	Meat Extract.	A pinch of ground
	2 tablespoonsful flour.	mace.

Boil the cauliflower. Heat 1½ oz. butter and 2 tablespoonsful flour to a golden brown, add the cream and ½ pint of the water in which the cauliflower has been boiled, with half a teaspoonful Meat Extract dissolved in it. Boil this sauce till thick, then flavour with ground mace. Strain and pour over the cauliflower, which has been placed in a deep dish. Melt the remaining 1 oz. butter, pour it over, sprinkle with grated Parmesan cheese, and bake in a hot oven, standing the dish in a pan of boiling water.

Schwarzwurzeln
(Salsify.)

Wash, dry and scrape the roots, throwing each at once into water, in which a tablespoonful of flour and of vinegar have been stirred, so as to retain a good colour. When all have been scraped, take them out, rinse them in fresh cold water and then throw them into slightly salted boiling water, to which a very little sugar may be added. When tender, take out, drain on a sieve and treat as asparagus and cauliflower, serving with brown butter, various sauces, or bake.

Reckon from 30 to 40 heads of salsify for every 6 persons.

In South Germany, the salsify is frequently dipped in batter and fried a pale golden colour in a saucepanful of frying fat or butter.

Spinat
(Spinach.)

For 6 Persons.   *Time of Preparation: 2 hours.*

6 lbs. spinach.	½ pint stock.	½ teaspoonful chopped
4 oz. butter.	2 tablespoonsful flour.	onion or chives.
4 Sardellen.		Salt and pepper.

Wash and pick the spinach thoroughly. Throw it into 2 quarts of boiling water, containing 1 tablespoonful of salt and 1 teaspoonful carbonate of soda. Bring to the boil, then draw on one side. Repeat this three times, then shake out on to a sieve, leave to drain for a few minutes and chop finely.

Brown half the quantity of the butter with the flour in a saucepan, add the chopped spinach, onion or chives, and the remaining butter and then the stock, stirring continually till the whole has boiled up well. Finally add the Sardellen, finely chopped, and pepper and salt to taste.

Serve garnished with slices of hard-boiled eggs or Sardellen.

Schoten
(Green Peas.)

For 6 Persons.   *Time of Preparation: 1 hour.*

2 lbs. green peas.	1 tablespoonful flour.	Sugar and salt to taste.
2 oz. butter,	1 tablespoonful	
¾ pint stock.	chopped parsley.	

Boil the peas in the stock till tender with 1 oz. butter and a little salt and sugar. Mix the remaining oz. of butter with the flour to a ball and boil it with the peas till dissolved. Then flavour with sugar and salt to taste and, just before serving, stir in the chopped parsley.

Schoten mit Reis. — Rizi Pizi
(Green Peas with Rice.)

For 6 Persons.   *Time of Preparation: 1¼ hour.*

1 lb. green peas.	1 teaspoonful chopped parsley.
3 oz. butter.	1½ pint stock.
4 oz. rice.	Sugar and salt to taste.

Scald the rice and boil it till soft with half the quantity of the stock and butter. Boil the peas in the remaining stock and butter, and when tender, stir carefully, with the parsley, into the rice. Add sugar and salt to taste, and serve.

Schoten mit Reis und Tomaten
(Green Peas with Rice and Tomatoes.)

Proceed as in last recipe. To the ingredients there named, take 4 medium-sized tomatoes. Skin them, cut them into slices and stew them for 5 minutes in 1 oz. butter, with ½ teaspoonful chopped onion.

Rub through a sieve and add with the parsley to the peas, when the latter are already tender. Flavour with sugar and lemon juice and stir into the rice.

The tomato purée may also be mixed only with the rice, which should then be placed in the middle of the dish and the peas arranged round it, the chopped parsley being sprinkled over the whole.

Schoten und Mohrrüben
(Green Peas and Carrots.)

For 6 Persons.   *Time of Preparation: 1½ hour.*

1 lb. peas.	¾ pint stock.	1 tablespoonful flour.
2 oz. butter.	Salt.	2 tablespoonsful
1 oz. sugar,	1½ lb. carrots.	chopped parsley.

Scrape and wash the carrots and cut them up into small dice. Boil with the peas, till tender, in the broth, with 1½ oz. butter, sugar and salt. Mix the remaining butter and the flour to a ball and boil it with the vegetables till dissolved. On serving, stir in the chopped parsley.

Tiny spring carrots may be taken instead of ordinary carrots. In this case, boil carrots and peas separately in the stock, with salt, sugar and a little parsley. Serve the carrots in the middle of the dish, the peas arranged round them, and parsley sprinkled over the whole.

Karotten
(Carrots.)

For 6 Persons.   *Time of Preparation: 1½ hour.*

2 lbs. spring carrots.	1 tablespoonful chopped parsley.
3 oz. butter.	1 tablespoonful flour.
¾ pint, stock.	Salt and sugar to taste.

Scrape and wash the carrots and stew them gently, till tender, in the stock, with 2 oz. of the butter and a little sugar. Mix the remaining butter and the flour to a ball and boil it with the carrots till dissolved. Stir in the chopped parsley just before serving, and add sugar and salt to taste.

Grune Bohnen
(French Beans.)

For 6 Persons.   *Time of Preparation: 2 hours.*

2 lbs. beans.	1 tablespoonful	1¼ pint stock.	A little sugar.
2 oz. butter.	flour.	Fresh herbs.	Salt.

Wash and string the beans, cut into thin strips, or merely break across into two or three pieces. Scald them, and then put on in the boiling stock, with 1½ oz. butter and some fresh herbs (Pfefferkraut), to boil gently till tender.

Brown the remaining butter with the flour and add to the beans. Just before serving, stir in the chopped parsley and add sugar and salt to taste.

Grüne Bohnen mit Mohrrüben
(French Beans with Carrots.)

Prepare as Peas and Carrots (*see* recipe), scalding the beans first and allowing 1½ lb. carrots to 1 lb. finely-cut beans.

Grüne Bohnen mit Milch
(French Beans with Milk.)

For 6 Persons.   *Time of Preparation: 2 hours.*

1 tablespoonful chopped parsley.	2 oz. butter.
½ teaspoonful Liebig's Meat Extract.	1½ pint milk.
A pinch of nutmeg.	1 tablespoonful flour.
2 lbs. beans.	Fresh herbs.

Boil the beans (either cut, or broken in short lengths) with salt until tender, then drain on a sieve. Brown the butter and flour slightly, stir in the milk and a little Meat Extract, boil up, add a pinch of nutmeg, the chopped parsley, herbs (Pfefferkraut), salt, and finally the beans, bring all once more to the boil and serve.

Grüne Bohnen mit Birnen
(French Beans with Pears. — A Frisian dish.)

For 6 Persons.   *Time of Preparation: 2 hours.*

1½ lb. beans.	3 oz. butter	Lemon juice.	1 tablespoonful
1 lb. pears.	¾ pint stock.	Sugar.	flour.

String the beans and either cut them into thin strips or break them into short lengths. Scald them and then put them on in boiling stock with salt and half of the butter. When nearly tender, add the pears peeled and cut into quarters and continue boiling until both pears and beans are quite tender. Before adding the pears, slightly brown the remainder of the butter with the flour and add to the beans. Flavour with lemon juice and sugar.

Grüne Bohnen mit Tomaten
(French Beans with Tomatoes.)

For 6 Persons. *Time of Preparation:* 2 hours.

2 lbs. beans.	1 teaspoonful flour.	A pinch of carbonate of
1 lb. tomatoes.	1 tablespoonful lemon	soda.
2 oz. butter,	juice,	½ teaspoonful chopped
1¼ pint stock.	1½ oz. chopped ham.	onion.
A little sugar.	1 tablespoonful	1 tablespoonful vinegar.
Salt.	chopped parsley.	

String the beans, break them across into short lengths, put them on in boiling water with 1 tablespoonful vinegar and a pinch of carbonate of soda. Bring to the boil, pour this water away and then boil till tender in the stock with 1 oz. of the butter.

Cut the tomatoes into slices, dredge over with flour and stew gently in a covered saucepan for 10 minutes, with the chopped ham and an oz. of butter. Add the onion to the stock in which the beans have been boiled, which should now amount to about ½ pint. Boil a further 5 minutes and pour the thick sauce so obtained through a hair sieve on to the beans, which must then be allowed once more to boil up.

Flavour with lemon juice and sugar, stir in the chopped parsley and serve.

Green peas can be prepared with tomatoes in the same way.

Buntes Gemüse
(Leipziger Allerlei.)

For 6 Persons. *Time of Preparation:* 3 hours.

4 oz. shelled green peas.	½ oz. parsley root, chopped.
8 oz. asparagus, cut into short lengths.	2 oz. butter.
	1 tablespoonful sugar.
4 oz. cauliflower, divided into tiny heads.	1 tablespoonful chopped parsley.
	1 tablespoonful flour.
4 oz. small spring carrots.	Sugar and salt to taste.
4 oz. kohlrabi, sliced.	

Boil each vegetable separately in slightly salted water. Slightly brown 1 oz. butter and the flour in a saucepan, add 1 pint of the water in which the asparagus has been boiled and the chopped parsley root. Boil up this sauce well and flavour with a little sugar. Then put into it all the various vegetables, keeping back some of each kind, with which to garnish the dish, and finally adding the chopped green parsley. The dish may be further improved by the addition of little meat balls, or slices of tongue, arranged as a border round the dish, with alternate little heaps of the vegetables that have been held over for garnishing.

Kohlrabi

For 6 Persons.　　　　　*Time of Preparation:* 2 hours.

3 lbs. kohlrabi.	1 tablespoonful flour.	A little sugar.
1¼ pint stock.	1 tablespoonful	A pinch of pepper.
¾ oz. butter.	chopped parsley.	A pinch of salt.

Pick off the leaves from the stalks, wash them well, boil them in salted water till tender, then pour off the water, rinse the leaves in cold water and chop finely.

Peel the roots, cut them into slices, scald them and boil in stock or mutton broth, till soft.

Brown the butter and flour slightly in a saucepan, add the sliced vegetable, the chopped leaves, salt, pepper and sugar to taste and allow to simmer for 5 minutes. Just before serving, stir in the chopped parsley.

Kohlrabi mit Milchsauce
(Kohlrabi with Milk Sauce.)

For 6 Persons.　　　　　*Time of Preparation:* 2 hours.

3 lbs. kohlrabi,	2 oz. butter.	A little sugar.
¾ pint milk.	1 tablespoonful flour.	Pepper and salt to taste.

Prepare the leaves as in preceding recipe. Peel and slice the roots and boil with salt and 1 oz. butter in sufficient water just to cover them. Then take out and drain on a sieve.

Slightly brown the remainder of the butter with the flour, add 1 pint of the water in which the kohlrabi has been boiled and the milk and bring to the boil. Into this thickened sauce put the chopped leaves and the sliced kohlrabi and simmer gently for 5 minutes, adding pepper, salt and sugar to taste.

The addition of 4 oz. boiled potatoes, cut into slices, is an improvement.

Sellerie-Gemüse
(Celery Root.)

2 lbs. celery root.	2 tablespoonsful lemon	A pinch of salt.
2 oz. butter.	juice.	A pinch of pepper.
2 tablespoonsful flour.	1 teaspoonful sugar.	Sugar to taste.

Wash and brush the celery root thoroughly, then boil till tender in about 3 quarts water.

Brown the butter and the flour in a saucepan, add a pint of the water in which the celery was boiled and a little Meat Extract, boil up and flavour with sugar, lemon juice and pepper.

Peel the celery root, cut it into slices and boil up once in this sauce. It is an improvement to stir into the sauce the yolks of 2 beaten-up eggs.

Sellerie-Gemüse mit Sahnensauce
(Celery root with Cream Sauce.)

2½ lbs. celery root,	A little sugar.	1 tablespoonful lemon
1½ oz. butter.	2 tablespoonsful flour.	juice.
½ pint cream.	2 oz. chopped raw ham.	A pinch of pepper.

Prepare the celery root as in preceding recipe. Brown the butter and flour in a saucepan, add 1 pint of the water in which the celery has been boiled and the chopped ham, and boil the sauce well. Then add the cream, strain through a sieve, flavour with salt, pepper, sugar and lemon juice, place in it the sliced celery, boil up again once, and serve.

Pastinaka
(Parsneps.)

For 6 Persons.   *Time of Preparation:* 2 hours.

2½ lbs. parsneps.	1 oz. butter.	A pinch of salt.
½ pint stock.	1 tablespoonful flour.	
½ pint cream.	A pinch of pepper.	

Wash and scrape the parsneps, cut them into slices, and boil them with salt, till tender. Then drain on a sieve. Brown the butter and flour in a saucepan. Then add the stock and cream, salt and pepper to taste, and boil the sauce well. Place in it the slices of parsnep and simmer gently for another 5 minutes.

Geschmorte Gurken
(Stewed Cucumbers.)

For 6 Persons.   *Time of Preparation:* 2½ hours.

6 lbs. cucumbers.	2 oz. sugar.	1 teaspoonful potato
½ oz. onion.	2 tablespoonsful flour.	flour.
2 oz. butter,	1 tablespoonful salt.	½ gill wine vinegar.
1¼ pint stock.		A pinch of pepper.

Peel the cucumbers and cut into pieces lengthwise, removing all seeds. Sprinkle with salt and pepper and a little vinegar, and stand in a cool place, covered over, for one hour.

Then boil in the stock till tender, with the juice that has come from them while standing, a little vinegar and the onion.

Melt the butter in a saucepan and brown it with the flour and a little sugar, add the cucumber stock and boil this sauce well. Then put in the cucumber and simmer for another 10 minutes. Finally stir the potato flour smoothly in a little water and add to the sauce to thicken it, flavouring with sugar and vinegar to taste.

Gefüllte Gurken
(Stuffed Cucumbers.)

For 6 Persons.   Time of Preparation: 3 hours.

4 lbs. cucumbers.	¾ lb. pork.	Other ingredients as in
1 oz. breadcrumbs,	1 egg	preceding recipe.

Peel the cucumbers, cut them in halves, remove the seeds, and leave them to stand for an hour, covered, sprinkled over with pepper, salt and vinegar. Then parboil them carefully.

With the finely-chopped pork, the breadcrumbs, an egg and salt make mincemeat and fill the cavities of the cucumbers with it. Fit the halves together again, tie them together and stew as in last recipe, preparing the sauce in the same manner.

Rote Rüben
(Beetroot.)

For 6 Persons.   *Time of Preparation:* 4 hours.

4 lbs. beetroot.	2 ground cloves.	1 teaspoonful ground
2 oz. butter.	3 tablespoonsful sour	carraway seeds.
1 gill stock.	cream.	1 tablespoonful flour.
1 gill wine vinegar.		

| 1 teaspoonful chopped | onion. | Sugar and salt to taste. |

Wash and boil the beetroot till tender. Remove the skin and cut into thin slices.

Brown the butter and flour in a saucepan; add to them the stock, spices and onion, and boil all up together. Then add the sliced onion, flavour with vinegar and sugar, and allow all to simmer for a few minutes. Add finally the cream thickened with a little flour, and serve.

Two tablespoonsful of grated horseradish may also be added just before serving.

Geschmorte Maronen
(Stewed Chestnuts.)

For 6 Persons. Time of Preparation: 1½ hour.

2 lbs. chestnuts.	½ gill red wine.	1 tablespoonful lemon
2 oz. butter.	½ teaspoonful potato	juice.
½ pint stock.	flour,	
A little sugar.		

Remove the hard brown skin of the chestnuts with a knife, and then put them into boiling water until the yellow skin can be easily peeled off.

Brown the butter with a little sugar in a saucepan, and add to it the stock and lemon juice. Place the chestnuts in this and stew them until tender, adding then the red wine, or 3 tablespoonsful of Madeira, thickened with flour.

Maronen mit Aepfeln
(Chestnuts with Apples.)

| 1 lb. chestnuts. | 1½ lb. apples. | Sugar to taste. |

Remove both skins from the chestnuts (*see* preceding recipe) and boil with salt till tender.

Stew the apples with sugar, pass them through a sieve and serve mixed with the chestnuts.

Maronenpurée
(Chestnut purée.)

| 2 lbs. chestnuts. | A little sugar. | ½ gill sweet cream. |
| 2 oz. butter. | ¾ pint veal stock. | A pinch of pepper. |

Remove both skins from the chestnuts (see recipe on previous page) and boil in the stock till quite soft. Rub through a sieve, then stir briskly over the fire with the butter and cream, flavouring with sugar and pepper. This dish is an excellent addition to Sauerkohl.

Erbsen
(Dried Peas.)

For 6 Persons.　　　　　　　*Time of Preparation:* 2 hours.

1½ lb. yellow or green dried peas, 1½ oz. butter.	Salt. 1 onion. 2½ pints stock.	Soup herbs (carrots, turnips, parsley root, celery).

Soak the peas overnight. Put them on to boil in cold water with a little carbonate of soda, and after they have boiled for 15 minutes pour off this water and fill up the saucepan with the stock, adding the soup herbs and onion, and boiling until quite soft. Then remove the soup herbs, rub the peas through a sieve, add the butter and stir well (but not directly over the fire) till thoroughly hot.

This dish may be varied by the addition of rice, ½ lb. rice being reckoned to every pound of peas. The rice should be scalded and added to the peas when they have been boiling in the stock for a short time.

Saure Bohnen oder Linsen
(Piquant Beans or Lentils.)

For 6 Persons.　　　　　　　*Time of Preparation:* 3 hours.

1½ lb. haricot beans or lentils. 3 oz. bacon.	1 onion. 2½ pints stock. 1 tablespoonful flour.	Vinegar. Sugar and salt.

Soak the lentils or haricots overnight, then put them on in cold water and boil for half an hour with a little carbonate of soda. Drain off the water, rinsing with fresh hot water and then continue boiling in the stock with an onion till soft. Cut the bacon into small dice and fry till the fat has nearly all run out, brown the flour in this and add to the lentils or beans, boiling a few minutes longer. Flavour with sugar, salt and sufficient vinegar to give the dish a piquant taste.

Bohnen oder Linsen mit Backpflaumen
(Haricots or Lentils with Prunes.)

1 lb. haricots or lentils.	1 lb. prunes.

Prepare the lentils or haricots according to preceding recipe. Stone and stew the prunes and boil them a short time with the lentils.

Wirsingkohl
(Savoy Cabbage.)

For 6 Persons.   *Time of Preparation: 2* hours.

4 lbs. Savoy cabbage.	2 tablespoonsful flour.	½ teaspoonful chopped
2 oz. butter.	A pinch of carbonate of	onion.
1¼ pint stock.	soda.	Salt.
A pinch of nutmeg.		

Remove the outer leaves, cut the heads into quarters, taking out the thick stalk. Wash and boil till tender with salt and a pinch of carbonate of soda, then take out and drain.

Brown the butter, flour and onion, add to them the stock and boil up to make a sauce, flavouring it with a pinch of nutmeg.

Place the Savoy in this sauce and then allow it to simmer gently for 15 minutes before serving.

Wirsing mit Milchsance
(Savoy Cabbage with Milk Sauce.)

5 lbs. Savoy.	A small onion.	A pinch of salt.
¾ pint milk.	2 tablespoonsful flour.	A pinch of nutmeg.
2 oz. butter.	A pinch of pepper.	

Prepare the Savoy as in preceding recipe and parboil it with an onion and salt; then press the water out of it. Brown the butter and the flour in a saucepan, add the milk, pepper and nutmeg and pour over the Savoy. Then stew in this sauce till tender.

Weisskobl
(Whiteheart Cabbage.)

This is prepared in a similar way to Savoy or Wirsingkohl, mutton broth being substituted for the beef stock and ground carraway seeds and a little sugar being added.

Gebackener Wirsing oder Weisskohl
(Baked Cabbage or Savoy.)

This is prepared in the same manner as baked cauliflower (*see* recipe) and is an excellent dish.

Reckon 3 lbs. of cabbage and a pint of sauce for every 6 persons.

Wirsingkohl auf süddeutsche Art
(South German preparation of Savoy.)

Boil the Savoy in salted water till soft, then chop up finely and stir in some butter, a pinch of pepper, 2 teaspoonsful chopped chives, J teaspoonful Meat Extract and a little cream. Serve very hot.

Gefüllter Weisskohl oder Wirsing
(Stuffed Cabbage or Savoy.)

For 6 Persons.   *Time of Preparation:* 2½ hours.

2 lbs. cabbage.	Salt and pepper.	1½ oz. bacon.
1 lb. pork.	1¼ pint stock.	Nutmeg.
1 oz. breadcrumbs.	2 tablespoonsful flour.	

Cut the cabbage or Savoy in half, parboil it with salt and place on a sieve to drain.

With the finely chopped pork, an egg, breadcrumbs, salt and pepper, make forcemeat and form it into a dozen little balls. Detach from the cabbage two large outer leaves and a few small inner ones. Place the outer leaves on a clean cloth, the little ones on them, and on these the forcemeat balls. Wrap the leaves carefully round, then press the cloth firmly over on all sides, so that it keeps well together. Remove the cloth and place the stuffed cabbage ball in a stewpan lined with strips of bacon. Repeat this proceeding until the forcemeat balls have been all wrapped round with cabbage leaves.

Make a pale sauce by slightly browning the butter and flour, adding the stock and boiling up. Pour this upon the stuffed cabbage balls and stew gently for about ¾ hour.

For whiteheart cabbage, flavour the sauce with nutmeg, for Savoy, with carraway.

The beaten-up yolks of 2 eggs and lemon juice may also be added to the sauce if preferred to other flavouring.

Grünkohl
(Broccoli.)

For 6 Persons.   *Time of Preparation:* 3 hours.

Carbonate of soda.	3 lbs. broccoli, picked over and
1 oz. fine semolina.	stalks removed.
3 ground cloves.	4 oz. butter,
½ teaspoonful chopped onion.	1¼ pint stock.
Salt.	

Pick over the greens, removing all stalk and wash thoroughly. Throw into boiling water and boil for about 30 minutes with plenty of salt and 1 tea-spoonful carbonate of soda. Drain well and then chop up finely.

Melt the butter in a saucepan, place the greens in it and pour some of the stock over it. Add the ground cloves and chopped onion and sprinkle the semolina over. Stew gently for 2 hours, adding the rest of the broth at inter-vals. For a **Bavarian variation**, boil the broccoli, strain and serve with small lumps of butter among it. Dust over with hard-boiled yolks, rubbed through a sieve.

Rosenkohl
(Brussels Sprouts.)

For 6 Persons.   *Time of Preparation:* 2 hours.

3 lbs. Brussels sprouts.	1 tablespoonful flour.	A pinch of nutmeg.
A pinch of carbonate of soda.	Salt.	1 teaspoonful chopped onion.
3 oz. butter.	1 pint stock.	
A pinch of pepper.	1 teaspoonful chopped parsley.	

Throw the sprouts, after removing the outer leaves, into 3 quarts boiling water, with salt and a pinch of carbonate of soda. After bringing up to the boil again, take the sprouts out and drain on a sieve and then on a dry cloth, so that no water remains in them.

Brown an oz. of the butter with the flour and sugar, add the stock, chopped onion and parsley, pepper, nutmeg and the remaining butter. Boil up well, then put in the sprouts and allow all to simmer gently for ½ hour.

Rosenkohl gebacken
(Baked Brussels Sprouts.)

For 6 Persons.   *Time of Preparation:* 2 hours.

Ingredients as in last recipe. Boil the sprouts till tender and drain on a sieve. Prepare the sauce similarly and boil down to ½ pint. Beat the yolk of 1 egg and a gill of sour cream well together, thicken with ½ teaspoonful flour and add to the sauce.

Fill a china mould with the sprouts, pour over them the sauce, sprinkle grated roll and Parmesan cheese on top and bake 15 minutes in a hot oven.

Rotkohl
(Red Cabbage.)

For 6 Persons.   *Time of Preparation:* 2 hours.

4 lbs. cabbage.	2 teaspoonsful ground	Vinegar.
4 oz. lard.	carraway seed.	Salt.
2 oz. sugar.	½ teaspoonsful chopped	
1 pint water.	onion.	
1 potato.	2 apples *or* pears.	

Cut the cabbage up finely, scald it with boiling water, drain off and pour on at once 2 tablespoonsful vinegar. Melt the lard and stir it into the cabbage. Cut the apples or pears into slices and add, with the chopped onion, ground carraway seed and salt. Pour over ½ pint water and simmer for 1½ to 2 hours. Then add the sugar and a grated raw potato and serve.

Bayrisch Kraut

Prepared in the same way as Rotkohl, but with Weisskohl (whiteheart cabbage) or a mixture of the red and white cabbage.

Gekochte Kartoffeln in verschiedenen Saucen
(*Boiled Potatoes with Various Sauces.*)

The sauce for a potato dish should be made somewhat thinner than usual as the potatoes thicken it.

Boil the potatoes in their skins, cut them into slices, place, still warm, in any of the following sauces: Parsley, Bechamel, Onion, Mustard, or Fricassee, for a few minutes and then serve.

Reckon 1¼ pint of sauce to every 2 lbs. of potatoes.

Brühkartoffeln
(Potatoes Boiled in Stock.)

For 6 Persons.   *Time of Preparation:* 1¼ hour.

3 lbs. peeled potatoes.	1 teaspoonful carraway seed
2 sliced onions.	1¼ pint stock.
Some peppercorns	1 tablespoonful chopped parsley.

Peel and wash the potatoes, cut into quarters, and parboil. Then strain off the water and finish boiling in the stock, which has been previously well boiled with the onions, peppercorns and carraway seed.

Just before serving, add the chopped parsley.

Bruhkartoffeln mit Tomaten

For 6 Persons.   *Time of Preparation:* 1 hour.

3 lbs. potatoes.	Salt.	1 tablespoonful parsley.
3 oz. butter.	1¼ pint stock.	
3 oz. onions.	1¼ lb. tomatoes.	

Peel the potatoes and cut up into pieces lengthwise. Parboil in water with salt, then drain off and finish boiling in the stock.

Melt the butter and stew the tomatoes and onions in it. Rub through a sieve and add to the potatoes. On serving, sprinkle over with parsley.

Branne Petersilienkartoffeln
(Potatoes, Browned, with Parsley.)

For 6 Persons.   *Time of Preparation:* 1½ hour.

2 lbs. potatoes.	1 tablespoonful flour.	½ teaspoonful Meat Extract.
1 oz. butter,	1 tablespoonful chopped parsley.	
¾ pint cream.		
A pinch of pepper.		

Peel and slice the potatoes. Boil them and then drain well. Stir the Meat Extract, flour and pepper into the cream and pour over the potatoes. Add the butter and some salt and boil for 3 minutes.

Stir in the chopped parsley and serve with cutlets, chops, rissoles, etc.

Kartoffeln mit Tomatensauce
(Potatoes with Tomato Sauce.)

For 6 Persons.   *Time of Preparation:* 1½ hour.

1½ lb. potatoes.	2 oz. onions.	Salt to taste.
1 quart stock.	2 tablespoonsful flour.	
3 oz. butter.	A few tomatoes.	

Boil the potatoes in their skins, then peel and slice them. Melt the butter in a saucepan and heat the sliced onions in it for 3 minutes. Then add the tomatoes and flour, and after another 5 minutes, the stock and boil till the tomatoes are quite soft. Rub through a sieve, salt to taste and pour over the slices of potatoes, while the latter are still warm, boiling up once again before serving.

Kartoffeln mit Aepfeln
(Potatoes with Apples.)

For 6 Persons.   *Time of Preparation:* 1½ hour.

2 lbs. potatoes.	2 lbs. apples.
2 oz. bacon.	Sugar and salt to taste.

Peel the potatoes, cut into quarters, boil with salt, drain and partly mash. Meanwhile boil the apples to a pulp and then mix well with the potatoes, flavouring with salt and sugar. Cut the bacon into dice, fry until the fat is melted and pour over the dish. In some districts, fresh plums, prunes and pears are prepared with potatoes in the same way.

Heringskartoffeln
(Herring Potatoes.)

For 6 Persons.   *Time of Preparation:* 1½ hour.

2 lbs. potatoes boiled in their skins.	A pinch of pepper.	1 tablespoonful flour.
1¼ pint milk or cream.	2 oz. butter.	½ teaspoonful chopped onion.
	2 pickled herrings.	

Brown the butter and flour slightly, add the milk, and boil up to make a thick sauce. Then add the chopped onion and pepper, and finally the pickled herrings (which should have been well soaked and then chopped finely) and the potatoes cut into slices. Draw on one side and simmer for 5 minutes, then add salt if necessary, and serve.

Gebackene Heringskartoffeln
(Baked Herring Potatoes.)

2 lbs. potatoes boiled in their skins.	4 pickled herrings.
2 yolks of eggs.	¾ pint sour cream.
2 oz. butter.	1 oz. Parmesan cheese.

Butter a china mould and place in the bottom of it a layer of sliced boiled potatoes, then a layer of herring, cut into dice after having been soaked, then again potatoes, and continue the alternate layers till the mould be full, the top layer being potatoes.

Pour over this the yolks and the cream well beaten together, place the butter in lumps on the top, sprinkle the grated Parmesan cheese over it, and bake 30 minutes. Slices of pickled cucumber may be added in the layers of potatoes.

Saure Kartoffeln
(Piquant Potatoes.)

For 6 Persons.   *Time of Preparation:* 1½ hour.

2 lbs. potatoes.	1 Vinegar.
¼ tablespoonful flour.	Sugar and salt to taste.
1 lb. bacon.	

Boil the potatoes in their skins. Cut the bacon into dice and put into a saucepan on a good fire until the fat has melted. Then brown the flour in it with a little sugar, add water, and boil up to make a thickish sauce. Place the potatoes, cut into thick slices, into this, bring once more to the boil, flavour with vinegar, salt and sugar, and serve.

Schinken-Kartoffeln
(Ham Potatoes.)

Boil and peel the potatoes and cut into slices. Mix with some minced ham and a thick savoury sauce. Sprinkle a little Parmesan cheese on top, and bake to a nice brown.

Hamburgische Kartoffeln
(Hamburg Potatoes.)

1 oz. butter.	½ lb. potatoes.
Pepper and salt.	2 eggs.

Bake half a pound of potatoes in their skins, remove the latter, and rub the potatoes through a wire sieve.

Put them in a saucepan with the butter, pepper and salt, then stir in, over the fire, the yolks of 2 eggs. Take off the fire, and add lightly the whipped whites of the 2 eggs. Have a pan of fat quite hot on the fire, and when it smokes put in a teaspoonful of the mixture, and fry it a light brown.

Scoop the mixture out of the spoon with another of the same size. To keep the balls a good shape, the spoons should be dipped into hot water each time they are used.

Kartoffelkugeln zum Garnieren
(Potato Balls for Garnishing.)

½ lb. boiled potatoes.	Breadcrumbs.
2 tablespoonsful flour.	2 eggs.
¾ oz. butter.	Salt.

Boil the potatoes, rub them through a sieve and stir into them 1 egg, beaten up, 2 tablespoonsful flour, ¾ oz. butter and salt.

Form little balls out of the mixture, roll them in egg and breadcrumbs and fry in butter.

Eartoffelring
(Potato Ring.)

For 6 Persons.   *Time of Preparation:* 2 hours.

1 lb. potatoes. | 2 eggs.
2 oz. butter. | Salt.

Boil and mash the potatoes, stir into them the butter, 2 beaten-up eggs and some salt and fill a well-buttered ring-shaped mould with the mixture. Bake a delicate brown. Turn out and serve with Sauerkohl or Ragout in the centre.

Sauerkraut

When freshly taken from the cask, press a little of the moisture out. Take half quantities of butter and lard, boil them with water in an earthenware pan and place the Sauerkraut in this, with a few slices of apple and an onion, a little sugar and salt. Cover closely and boil briskly till done, for 1½ to 2 hours.

Just before serving, stir in some mashed potatoes and a glass of light white wine.

Eierspeisen
(*Egg Dishes.*)

Eierkäse.   Eierziege.
(Eggcheese.)

For the Sauce:

8 eggs.	1 pint cream.	4 yolks.
1 1 pint cold milk.	3 oz. sugar.	1 tablespoonful cold milk.
1 oz. sugar.	A small stick of cinna-	
A little lemon juice.	mon.	½ teaspoonful potato flour.
A pinch of salt.	Rind of a lemon.	

Beat 8 eggs with 1½ pint cold milk, a few drops of lemon juice, 1 oz. sugar, a pinch of salt and pass twice through a hair sieve. Stir over the fire until it begins to curdle, then remove at once, stir another minute and pour into a mould, well rinsed with cold water.

To make the sauce, take 1 pint cream and boil it with 3 oz. sugar, a small stick of cinnamon and the rind of a lemon. Beat up 4 yolks with 1 tablespoonful cold milk, thickened with half a teaspoonful potato flour, and then mix well with the boiled cream. Turn out the shape when cold and pour the sauce over it.

Bunte Eier

6 hard-boiled eggs.	A pinch of pepper.
2 oz. Sardellen.	2 teaspoonsful chopped capers.
1½ oz. lobster, boiled ham ox-tongue.	1½ oz. PfefFergurken.
A few leaves of gelatine.	2 tablespoonsful Tarragon vinegar.
1 yolk, raw.	2 tablespoonsful oil.
1 teaspoonful chopped parsley.	4 tablespoonsful stock.

Boil the eggs hard. Cut off the tops and remove the whole of the eggs with a spoon, being careful not to break the shell. Cut the whites, 2 of the yolks, the Pfeffergurken, Sardellen and lobster (or ham, or tongue) into tiny dice. Beat up the raw yolk and mix it, with a pinch of salt, with the remaining hard-boiled yolks and the oil, then add the vinegar and the stock, in which a little gelatine has been dissolved. Put the empty shells into egg-cups and fill them with alternate layers of this sauce and of the other ingredients that have been cut into dice. As soon as the eggs are full, replace the tops that have been cut off.

When set, cut the eggs in half, lengthwise, and serve with lettuce salad.

Rühreier
(Scrambled Eggs.)

Reckon 1 tablespoonful of milk, a piece of butter, half the size of a walnut, and a little salt to each egg. Beat all well together and stir over a gentle fire till it thickens.

A piquant flavour is given to the eggs, if instead of butter and milk, water and bacon, cut into small dice, are taken.

Mushrooms cut up small, little cooked heads of asparagus, small pieces of Sardellen, or a few spoonsful of grated cheese may be added.

If served with cold tongue, sausage or smoked meat, the addition of a little finely-chopped chives to the beaten-up eggs is an improvement.

Rühreier in Muschelsohalen
(Scrambled Eggs in Scallops.)

For 6 Persons.   *Time of Preparation:* 2 hours.

Scrambled eggs made from 8 eggs.	A small bottleful of mushrooms.
½ teaspoonful Liebig's Meat Extract	2 oz. chopped boiled ham.
dissolved in 4 tablespoonsful cream.	1 oz. Parmesan cheese.
2 oz. butter.	Salt.
3 Sardellen.	Chopped parsley.

Chop the mushrooms and stew them for 4 minutes in the butter and cream with a little chopped parsley and the Meat Extract, and mix with the chopped ham and Sardellen.

Scramble the eggs and fill warmed scallop shells alternately with this mixture and the eggs. Sprinkle with Parmesan cheese and serve very hot.

Plinsen

4 tablespoonsful flour.	2 oz. currants.
4 eggs.	2 tablespoonsful oiled butter.
1 gill milk.	Grated lemon peel *or* nutmeg.
½ gill water, warm.	A little salt.

Mix all ingredients thoroughly, beat well and make out of this quantity 4 pancakes. Cut each in four, sprinkle with sugar and cinnamon, and roll together.

They may also be served as a sweet with a red or white wine sauce or a fruit sauce.

If served with spinach, omit the lemon peel, currants and sugar, and stir into the batter before frying, finely chopped chives.

Wasser-Eierkuchen
(Water Pancakes.)

¼ lb. flour.	3 whites of eggs.
½ pint water.	2 oz. butter.
3 yolks.	A little lemon peel and juice.

Mix well together the beaten-up yolks, water, salt and lemon peel, grated. Sift the flour, add the eggs and water gradually to it and beat well. Stir in finally the whites, whisked stiffly.

Fry a nice yellow in very hot fat and serve with sugar and lemon juice.

If fried in bacon fat, these pancakes are excellent with lettuce salad.

Verschiedene Arten Von Butter
(*Various Kinds of Butter.*)

Pikante-Butter
(Piquant Butter.)

2 small gherkins (Cornichons).	2 Sardellen.
½ teaspoonful German mustard.	2 oz. butter.
1 teaspoonful chopped parsley.	A small pinch of pepper.

Chop the Sardellen and gherkins very finely. Cream the butter and naix all well together.

116

Mostrich-Butter
(Mustard Butter.)

2 oz. butter.
2 hard-boiled yolks.

2 teaspoonsful German mustard.

Cream the butter, rub the yolks and mix all well together with the mustard.

Champignon-Butter
(Mushroom Butter.)

2 oz. butter.
2 oz. mushrooms.

A little finely chopped parsley.
A few drops lemon juice.

Chop up finely the mushrooms (either bottled or fresh ones stewed in a little butter), and stir them with the butter for 10 minutes. Then add the parsley and lemon juice. This is excellent spread on bread or rolls with lobster laid on it.

Hacksalat für Butterbrot
(Chopped Salad for Bread and Butter.)

1 herring, pickled.
1 tablespoonful oil.
1 apple.

1 tablespoonful vinegar.
Half a pickled cucumber.
1 grated horseradish.

An onion.
Pepper.
A little German mustard.

Soak the herring, dry it on a cloth and remove the bones. Peel the cucumber and remove the seeds. Chop up finely the herring, cucumber, and the peeled and cored apple, and mix with the other ingredients. Sardellen may be substituted for the herring and 4 oz. chopped roast meat or boiled ham added.

Spread this salad on bread, or rolls cut in half, garnishing with slices of hard-boiled egg.

Sardellen-Butter

4 oz. butter.

4 oz. Sardellen.

Cream the butter. Wash and bone the Sardellen, chop them up finely and stir into the butter.

Brötchen mit Sardellen-Butter

Spread the bread, or roll cut into half, with the Sardellen butter and scatter on it chopped smoked ham with hard-boiled eggs, cut into slices, placed on it.

Sardellenbrötchen

Cut the rolls in half, butter them and arrange Sardellen (soaked, dried and boned) across diagonally, from left to right and right to left. Fill the spaces with capers, chopped up hard-boiled eggs, chopped parsley or chives, small pieces of lobster, cold roast meat, ham, etc., as desired.

Krebs-Butter
(Crayfish Butter.)

| 12 crayfish. | ¼ lb. butter. |

Pick out the meat of a dozen freshly boiled crayfish. Pound the shells and claws in a mortar. Add the butter and pound all to a paste. Put into a stewpan and stir over a slow fire till the butter boils and becomes red. Then add a cupful of boiling water and simmer for a few minutes. Strain through a hair sieve into a jar and, when cold, skim the red butter off the top.

Salate
(*Salads.*)

Dressing for Various Salads

I. Mayonnaise

½ pint best salad oil.	1 gill best vinegar.	A pinch of white pepper.
2 yolks of eggs.	1 teaspoonful sugar.	1 tablespoonful
1 oz. flour.	½ teaspoonful German	chopped parsley.
1 gill stock.	mustard.	
1 gill water.	A pinch of cayenne.	

Stir 2 tablespoonsful oil and the flour well together in a saucepan, add the water and 1 tablespoonful vinegar and stir continuously. When this has boiled to a thick paste, remove from the fire and put into a basin, pouring over it a little cold water. Beat the 2 yolks well, adding gradually the remainder of the oil and vinegar, then stir in ½ teaspoonful German or English mustard and a pinch of cayenne and of white pepper. Pour the cold water off the paste in the basin, stir the latter quite smooth and mix it with the sauce just prepared, adding the sugar and chopped parsley. Finally thin the mayonnaise with a little stock or cream.

II. Weisse Mayonnaise
(White Mayonnaise.)

2 oz. fresh butter.	1 tablespoonful flour.	½ gill water.
1 gill oil.	½ teaspoonful mus-	A pinch of pepper.
1 gill Tarragon vinegar.	tard.	
1 teaspoonful sugar.	½ gill stock.	

Put 1 oz. butter and a tablespoonful flour in a saucepan and stir continuously, adding ½ gill water. When this has boiled down to a thick paste, remove from the fire and put into a basin, pouring over it a little cold water. Cream f oz. butter, place on ice or in very cold water, and stir in the oil, drop by drop, and then the vinegar, mustard and pepper.

Pour the cold water off the paste in the basin and stir the stock into it, mixing well and adding the sugar. Stir the prepared mayonnaise into it gradually and mix the whole well by continued stirring, adding salt and, if desired, a little cayenne to taste.

This mayonnaise is particularly suitable with potato salad.

III. Remonlade
(Remoulade Dressing.)

4 hard-boiled yolks.	1 tablespoonful German mustard.
1 gill best salad oil.	1 tablespoonful chopped parsley.
1 gill wine vinegar.	2 finely-chopped Sardellen.
½ gill stock.	1 finely-chopped shallot.
1 raw yolk.	

Pound the yolks in a mortar, then stir into the beaten-up raw yolk. Mix in gradually the oil, then the vinegar, stock and mustard till a thick sauce is formed. Season this with the addition of a tablespoonful of chopped parsley and a shallot and 2 Sardellen, finely chopped.

IV. Robe Batter-Sanoe
(Uncooked Butter Dressing.)

1 tablespoonful chopped parsley.	4 raw yolks.
A pinch of salt.	1 gill best salad oil.
A pinch of pepper.	1 gill vinegar.
A pinch of mustard.	1 teaspoonful capers.
1 oz. fresh butter.	

Cream the butter with the pepper and mustard and stir in gradually the beaten-up yolks, oil, vinegar and capers.

This sauce is suitable for potato salad or a mixed salad of potatoes and celery, or of potatoes and fish.

Kopfsalat — I.
(Lettuce or Endive Salad. — I.)

½ lb. picked-over lettuce.
½ gill best vinegar *or* lemon juice.
½ gill salad oil.

A pinch of salt.
A little sugar.

Pick over the leaves, wash several times in cold water, dry in a cloth, being careful not to crush them, and mix lightly with a dressing of oil, salt, a little sugar and vinegar or lemon juice. The lemon juice or vinegar should be added last.

The salad may be varied by the addition of chopped parsley, chives. Tarragon, dill, or borage, or slices of fresh cucumbers, and the sugar may be omitted if preferred. It is advisable to use for salad dressing, vinegar that has been boiled and allowed to cool again.

Lettuce Salad — II.

An agreeable variation to the lettuce salad is a dressing composed of vinegar, sugar and thick sour cream substituted for the oil.

Lettuce Salad — III.

Dress the lettuces with Mayonnaise Dressing No. I.

Lettuce Salad — IV.

Dress the lettuces with Salad Dressing No. IV, omitting the capers and substituting for them finely-chopped onion or chives.

Gurken-Salat
(Cucumber Salad.)

2 lbs. cucumber sliced thinly.
A pinch of salt.
1 teaspoonful sugar.

½ gill vinegar.
1 tablespoonful chopped parsley.

Slice the cucumber very thinly, sprinkle over it a little salt and sugar, then pour over it the vinegar, mix well and sprinkle over with pepper and chopped parsley. Salad oil may also be added or a gill of sour cream. Lemon juice may be substituted for the vinegar.

Salat yon sanren Gurken
(Pickled Cucumber Salad.)

2 lbs. pickled cucumber.
1 teaspoonful sugar.
½ teaspoonful chopped onion.
2 tablespoonsful lemon juice.

A pinch of pepper.
1 tablespoonful chopped parsley.
1 tablespoonful oil.

Cut the pickled cucumber (saure Gurken) in slices and mix well with a dressing of lemon juice, oil, chopped parsley, pepper and a little chopped onion.

Spapgel-Salat — I.
(Asparagus Salad — I.)

2 lbs. asparagus.
1 gill vinegar.
A little sugar.
A pinch of pepper.

4 tablespoonsful oil.
1 tablespoonful chopped parsley.
1 teaspoonful chopped Tarragon.

Peel the asparagus, break it into pieces about 2 inches long and boil till tender, with salt in the water. While still slightly warm, mix with the oil, vinegar, chopped parsley and Tarragon and a little pepper and sugar.

Asparagus Salad — II.

Boil the asparagus and let it get quite cold. Then mix with Mayonnaise Dressing No. I, adding a teaspoonful of chopped Tarragon, a tablespoonful chopped parsley, and, as a further improvement, lobster or crayfish may be added.

Asparagus Salad — III.

Boil the asparagus and when lukewarm, mix it with Remoulade Salad Dressing.

Schotenkörner-Salat
(Green Pea Salad.)

Boil the peas with salt and when cold mix with Mayonnaise Dressing No. I. This may be improved by the addition of lobster or crayfish.

Bunter Salat
(Mixed Salad.)

1 small cauliflower.
4 oz. French beans.
6 oz. small carrots.
½ lb. shelled peas.

½ lb. asparagus.
3 lbs. sliced pickled cucumber.
Mayonnaise Dressing No. I.

Boil all the vegetables in slightly salted water, separately. Boil the carrots whole and then slice them up. Mix all (with the exception of the cauliflower) with the sliced pickled cucumber (saure Gurke), pour over Mayonnaise Dressing No. 1 and garnish with the cauliflower, broken into little heads.

Karotten-Salat
(Carrot Salad.)

2 lbs. small carrots.
4 tablespoonsful oil.
½ gill vinegar.

1 tablespoonful stock.
1 tablespoonful chopped parsley.

A pinch of pepper and salt.

Wash and boil the carrots. Then scrape them and cut into thin slices. Mix with oil, vinegar, salt and pepper, and sprinkle over with chopped parsley.

Grüner Bohnen-Salat — I.
(French Bean Salad — I.)

1½ lb. beans.
4 tablespoonsful oil.
1 teaspoonful sugar.
1 teaspoonful chopped fresh herbs.
Vinegar to taste.

3 tablespoonsful water in which a little Liebig's Meat Extract is dissolved.
1 tablespoonful chopped parsley.
A pinch of pepper.

Cut up the beans finely and boil till tender with salt and a pinch of carbonate of soda. Drain on a sieve. Then pour over them first the oil and then the other ingredients of the dressing and mix thoroughly. The sugar may be omitted if preferred.

Bean Salad — II.

Prepare as in preceding recipe, serve in a dish with alternate layers of beans and thin slices of pickled cucumbers. Bean salad may also be mixed with sliced fish, cucumbers, potatoes, tomatoes or lettuce leaves.

Bean Salad — III.

Prepare the dressing as No. 1 recipe, adding 4 tablespoonsful sour cream and a little more pepper and omitting the onions.

Bean Salad — IV.

Cut the beans finely or break them into short lengths and mix them with Remoulade Dressing No. III.

Sellerie-Salat —I.
(Celery Salad — I.)

2 lbs. celery root.	1 tablespoonful stock.
4 tablespoonsful oil.	1 tablespoonful chopped parsley.
½ gill Vinegar.	½ teaspoonful chopped onion.
A little sugar.	A pinch of pepper.

Wash the celery root well, boil it with salt till tender, then peel and cut it into slices. Sprinkle with pepper and chopped onion and pour over the oil and vinegar, mixed with a little stock and sugar. Sprinkle with chopped parsley.

Slices of beetroot may be mixed with the celery.

Celery Salad — II.

Prepare celery as described and pour over the slices Mayonnaise Dressing No. I, mixed with a little chopped parsley.

Celery Salad — III.

Take half quantities of celery and sliced pickled cucumber, add a little watercress and pour over this Remoulade Salad Dressing No. III.

Kartoffel-Salat — I.
(Potato Salad — I.)

2 lbs. potatoes.	5 tablespoonsful oil.
½ gill vinegar.	1 tablespoonful chopped parsley.
Salt.	1 teaspoonful chopped onion.

If possible take special salad potatoes, procurable at most German Delicatessen shops. If these are not to be had, take the least floury ones possible. Boil them in their skins, peel while warm, and cut into slices.

Then mix at once with oil, vinegar, chopped onion and parsley, and allow to stand for about an hour before serving.

It is an improvement to pour a very little stock over the potatoes before mixing with the dressing. Capers may also be added.

The salad may be varied by taking 3 parts potatoes and 1 part sliced pickled cucumbers, *or,* 3 parts potatoes and 1 part sliced beetroot and 2 tablespoonsful grated horseradish, *or,* 1 part potatoes and 1 part celery root, sliced.

Potato Salad — II.

Prepare the potatoes as before, and when cold, sprinkle with pepper and pour over them Mayonnaise Dressing No. I. Finely-chopped watercress may be mixed with this salad, larger pieces and slices of hard-boiled eggs being used as a garnish.

Two parts of potato and 1 part of endive, with the same dressing poured over them, make a good salad.

Potato Salad — III.

Mix a few finely-chopped bottled mushrooms with the potatoes, and pour over them Remoulade Dressing No. III.

Potato Salad with Cucumber and Sour Cream

Take equal quantities of potatoes and thinly-sliced cucumber, and pour over them the following dressing: Flavour some good sour cream with salt, pepper, and a little vinegar. Stir into it finely-chopped parsley and chives and beat for 10 minutes to a very frothy dressing.

Blumenkohl-Salat — I.
(Cauliflower Salad — I.)

1 small cauliflower.	A pinch of salt.
4 tablespoonsful oil.	A pinch of pepper.
6 tablespoonsful vinegar.	A little sugar.
1 tablespoonful stock.	

Break the cauliflower into separate little heads, wash well, and boil with salt, being careful the little heads remain whole. Drain on a sieve and mix with a dressing composed of above ingredients.

Cauliflower Salad — II.

Prepare as in preceding recipe, and, when quite cold, pour over Mayonnaise Dressing No. I.

Cauliflower Salad — III.

Prepare the cauliflower as described, and, when quite cold, pour over it Salad Dressing No. IV.

Rosenkohl-Salat
(Brussels Sprouts Salad.)

Remove the outer loose leaves from 1½ lb. Brussels sprouts and boil with salt till tender. Then drain well and pour over Remoulade Dressing No. III.

This salad may be varied by taking 2 parts Brussels sprouts, 1 part celery root, boiled and cut into strips, and 1 part boiled, sliced potatoes and allowing double the quantity of Sardellen to the Remoulade Dressing.

Salat von roten Rüben
(Beetroot Salad.)

3 lbs. beetroot.	A pinch of pepper.
1 gill vinegar.	1 teaspoonful chopped horseradish.
1 tablespoonful oil.	A pinch of carraway seeds.
A pinch of sugar.	A pinch of carraway coriander.

Boil the beetroot till tender, being careful not to cut off the roots or any other portion before boiling, or the colour will be lost. Peel and slice the beetroot and mix with the above ingredients of the dressing.

This salad may be varied by taking 2 parts beetroot that has lain in vinegar, to 1 part sliced apple and 1 part sliced, boiled potatoes, and mixing them with oil, vinegar, and grated horseradish.

Rotkohl-Salat — I.
(Red Cabbage Salad — I.)

1½ lb. red cabbage.	1 teaspoonful chopped onion.
5 tablespoonsful oil.	A pinch of pepper.
1 gill vinegar.	A pinch of salt.
1 tablespoonful sugar.	

Cut up the cabbage finely and boil with salt, adding a little vinegar to the water. Drain on a sieve and then mix with oil, vinegar, finely-chopped onion, pepper and sugar. The vinegar should be boiled up and poured hot over the cabbage, and sugar should never be omitted.

Slices of boiled celery root and a few slices of apple may also be added.

Roher Rotkohl-Salat
(Salad of uncooked Red Cabbage.)

Cut up the cabbage finely, sprinkle it well with salt and leave it covered, in a warm place, for 45 minutes. Then press out the water, and mix with finely-chopped onion, oil and vinegar and a little sugar.

Slices of boiled potatoes, or of uncooked apples, or of both, may be added.

Schwarzwurzel-Salat — I
(Salsify Salad — I.)

3 lbs. salsify.
¼ gill vinegar.
4 tablespoonsful oil.

1 tablespoonful chopped parsley.
1 tablespoonful stock.
A pinch of pepper and salt.

Scrape the salsify roots, throwing them into flour and water, as each is scraped, to preserve the colour. Then break into pieces about J inch long, boil till tender, drain on a sieve and mix with a dressing composed of the above ingredients.

Salsify Salad — II.

Prepare the salsify roots as in preceding recipe and mix with Mayonnaise Dressing No. I, adding a little chopped parsley.

Tomaten-Salat — I.
(Tomato Salad. — I.)

1½ lb. tomatoes.
2 tablespoonsful oil.

3 tablespoonsful vinegar.
1 onion.

A pinch of salt.
A pinch of pepper.

Skin the tomatoes, cut them into slices with a very sharp knife and remove the seeds. Dust over each slice with salt and pepper, and sprinkle with 3 or 4 drops of oil. Then pour over the vinegar. Boil up an onion in a little Tarragon vinegar and pour the latter over the salad.

Tomato Salad. — II.

Prepare the tomatoes as described. Lay each slice separately in the dish, pouring over a little of the Remoulade Dressing No. Ill, from which the Sardellen have been omitted.

Meerrettig-Salat mit Aepfeln
(Horseradish and Apple Salad.)

½ lb. horseradish.
1 lb. apples.

1 tablespoonful oil.
2 oz. sugar.

1 gill vinegar.
Pepper.

Wash the horseradish well, grate it and mix it at once with the sugar and vinegar. Peel and slice the apples, sprinkle them over with oil and pepper, and mix well with the horseradish.

This is a suitable salad with boiled fresh beef.

Apfel-Salat
(Apple Salad.)

Peel and slice the apples and let them stand for a time in a mixture of oil, lemon juice and sugar. Cut some onions in slices, bring them to the boil in weak vinegar and water, and, when cold, mix with the apples.

Vinegar to taste may be added.

Apfel-Salat mit Bering oder Sardellen
(Apple Salad with Herrings or Sardellen.)

1 lb. apples.	4 oz. chopped Sardellen *or* pickled
2 hard-boiled eggs.	herrings.
½ teaspoonful chopped onion,	4 tablespoonsful salad oil.
½ gill vinegar.	1 teaspoonful capers.
	Sugar to taste.

Soak the herrings or Sardellen, then chop them finely and mix with the oil, vinegar, hard-boiled eggs (chopped finely) and the capers. Add the apples, cut into tiny dice, flavour with pepper and sugar, and mix all thoroughly.

Herings-Salat mit saurer Sahne
(Herring Salad with Sour Cream.)

4 pickled herrings.	½ lb. apples.
½ lb. boiled potatoes.	½ lb. pickled cucumbers.
1 teaspoonful chopped onion.	4 tablespoonsful vinegar.
1 teaspoonful sugar.	A good pinch of pepper.
Lemon juice to taste.	1 tablespoonful chopped parsley.
½ pint thick sour cream.	

Soak the herrings several hours, then cut them into slices, as well as the potatoes, cucumbers and apples. Beat the cream well with the vinegar, lemon juice, parsley, onion, pepper and sugar, and mix thoroughly with the cut-up salad ingredients.

Garnish with parsley and radishes.

Herings-Salat
(Herring Salad.)

4 pickled herring's.	8 tablespoonsful salad oil.
1 lb. pickled cucumbers.	2 Tarragon vinegar.
1 lb. apples.	1 teaspoonful German mustard.
A pinch of pepper.	1 tablespoonful chopped onion.
A pinch of ground ginger.	10 oz. boiled potatoes.

Soak the herrings 4 to 6 hours, changing the water frequently. Then skin them and cut up into small dice, pouring over them vinegar and 3 table-spoonsful water. Peel the potatoes, apples and pickled cucumbers, and cut also into dice. Mix all well together with the oil.

Tarragon vinegar, German mustard, ginger and chopped onion. Sprinkle over with pepper and add sugar if desired. The salad may be varied by the addition of hard-boiled eggs, beetroot that has been soaked in vinegar, and ½ lb. cold veal, all cut into small dice.

Italienischer Salat
(Italian Salad.)

½ lb. cold roast veal.	Mayonnaise Dressing No. I, prepared
½ lb. apples, peeled and cut into fine	with 3 yolks.
shreds.	½ lb. pickled cucumbers, peeled,
2 oz. boiled ham or tongue.	seeds cut out and shredded.
1 pickled herring or 3 oz. Sardellen.	3 oz. boiled salad potatoes.
A little sugar.	2 teaspoonsful capers.
Vinegar and stock as required.	1½ oz. boiled celery root.
	1½ oz. boiled carrots.

Soak the herring and then bone it, or the Sardellen, chop up quite finely and pour over 2 tablespoonsful each of vinegar and stock. Cut all other in-gredients into short, thin strips. Make a Mayonnaise Dressing according to recipe No. I, using 3 yolks. Mix with it first the herring (or Sardellen) and ca-pers, and then the mea , apples and cucumber and finally the potatoes, car-rots and celery. Mix thoroughly. Garnish with sliced pickled cucumbers, hard-boiled eggs or chopped ham.

Bielefelder Salat
(Bielefeld Salad.)

3 Neunaugen (smoked lampreys).	7 oz. Sardellen.
4 pickled herrings,	10 oz. cold roast veal.
½ lb. ox tongue.	6 slices beetroot.
4 oz. Senfgurken (pickled cucumber).	4 oz. cornichons (gherkins).
½ lb. boiled celery root.	4 oz. boiled carrots.
8 hard-boiled eggs.	Capers.

For the Dressing:

8 hard-boiled yolks.	½ pint salad oil.
1 tablespoonful German mustard.	½ gill red wine.
1 tablespoonful chopped parsley.	Vinegar to taste.
1 tablespoonful chopped onion.	Pepper.
½ gill stock.	A little sugar.

Soak the Sardellen and herrings, dry them on a cloth and then cut them into tiny dice. Slice the remaining ingredients thinly.

Rub the hard-boiled yolks, add the oil gradually to them and stir to a thick creamy sauce. Add the remaining ingredients of the dressing, mix well and then stir in the herring, Sardellen and other sliced ingredients of the salad.

Garnish with little heaps of finely-chopped ham, hard-boiled eggs or aspic.

Salat von Hühnerfleisch
(Chicken Salad.)

2 boiled chickens.	½ lb. tinned peas.
1 tablespoonful chopped parsley and chives.	Mayonnaise Dressing No. I, prepared with ¾ pint oil.
2 tablespoonsful lemon juice.	

Remove the meat from the bones and cut up into small pieces. Sprinkle over with lemon juice and stand on one side for 30 minutes. Then mix with the peas, stir the chopped parsley and chives into the mayonnaise and mix all well together.

Garnish with gherkins and tiny onions. Asparagus may be substituted for the peas.

Salat von Huhn und Hammer
(Chicken and Lobster Salad.)

1 chicken.	1 lb. tinned salmon.	Mayonnaise Dressing
½ lb. tinned peas.		No. I, (¾ pint oil).

This is an excellent salad. It is prepared according to the preceding recipe.

Fisch-Salat
(Fish Salad.)

2 lbs. fish.	1 tablespoonful chopped parsley.
6 tablespoonsful oil.	1 tablespoonful capers.
6 tablespoonsful vinegar.	1 tablespoonful chopped watercress.
4 hard-boiled eggs.	A pinch of pepper.
½ gill stock.	1 teaspoonful chopped chives.

Boil the fish and remove it from the bones. Cut into slices and sprinkle over with pepper. Mix the oil, vinegar, stock and chopped parsley, etc., and pour over the fish, leaving to stand for an hour. Season further if required. Six chopped Sardellen may also be mixed with the salad. Sprinkle over with capers and garnish with the chopped hard-boiled eggs.

Fish Salad with Mayonnaise

2 lbs. boiled fish. | 1 Mayonnaise Dressing No. 1.

Bone the fish, and cut up into small pieces. Pour over it the Mayonnaise Dressing, prepared with ½ pint oil, with some chopped fresh herbs mixed with it. Garnish with young lettuce leaves and little heaps of aspic.

Schinken-Salat
(Ham Salad.)

¾ lb. boiled ham. | 1 teaspoonful chopped chives.
6 oz. boiled potatoes. | 1 teaspoonful German mustard.
Mayonnaise Dressing No. II (double | ½ tablespoonful chopped parsley.
quantities). |

Cut the ham and potatoes into small dice, stir them into the white Mayonnaise, flavoured with German mustard, parsley and chives, and garnish with little inner leaves of lettuce or endive.

Illustrierte Gurke
(Ornamented Cucumber.)

Peel a pickled cucumber (Salzgurke), cut it in half lengthwise, remove the seeds and dry with a cloth. Fill the cavity with ham (cut into short, thin strips), hard-boiled eggs (cut into quarters), and a little chopped parsley. Pour some aspic over and stand in a cool place till set.

This may be varied by the substitution of chopped Sardellen, herring, salmon or veal.

Serve with Remoulade Dressing or Mayonnaise.

Süsser Salat
(Fruit Salad.)

½ lb. apples. | 7 oz. sugar. | 13 large oranges.

Peel, core and slice the apples. Peel the oranges carefully, scraping off all the white part of the skin from the fruit and slice thinly, removing all pips. Place alternate layers of apples and oranges in a glass dish, sprinkling each layer with sugar. The topmost layer should be of oranges. Allow to stand in a cool place for about an hour before serving.

This salad may be varied by the addition of bananas and tinned apricots, pears and pineapples all cut into dice and their juice added.

Süsser Danziger Salat
(Danzig Fruit Salad.)

Mix ½ lb. cranberries and ½ lb. various bottled fruits with ½ pint cream and a tablespoonful lemon juice and serve in a glass dish.

Auflaufe
(*Soufflés.*)

An Auflauf is baked in a special mould, in a moderate oven. In the absence of a special mould, any high fire-proof mould may be used. It must be well-buttered and lined with grated roll. Several sheets of paper should be laid on the mould when filled, the lowermost being buttered. The mould should be placed in a vessel of boiling water to prevent the bottom of the Auflauf becoming overbaked. Send to table with a serviette wrapped round. Serve with a fruit or wine sauce, unless a vanilla sauce is specified.

Einfacher Auflauf
(Simple Auflauf.)

For 6 Persons.   *Time of Preparation:* 1½ hour.

3 oz. butter.	½ pint milk.
3 oz. sugar.	1 teaspoonful salt.
3 oz. flour.	3 oz. grated sweet almonds.
6 eggs.	6 grated bitter almonds.

Cream the butter, add the almonds, salt, sugar and yolks and stir for 1¼ hour. Then add the milk, and flour gradually and finally the whites of eggs, whisked stiffly.   Fill a well-buttered mould (*see* general directions: "Auflauf") and bake ¾ hour.

This Auflauf may also be flavoured with vanilla or lemon, instead of almonds, or a pound of apples, cut into thin slices, or finely-chopped candied peel, or stoned cherries, or plums.

Soufflé
(Lemon Souffle. — I.)

For 6 Persons.   *Time of Preparation:* 1 hour.

6 yolks of eggs.	4 tablespoonsful lemon juice.
8 whites of eggs.	The grated rind of a lemon.
5 oz. castor sugar.	

Beat the yolks and sugar very thoroughly, then add the lemon juice and grated rind and stir in the whites of eggs, whisked stiffly. Fill a well-buttered shallow mould (*see* general directions: "Auflauf") and put at once into a rather hot oven. Bake 8 to 12 minutes and serve at once.

Zitronen-Auflauf
(Lemon Auflauf. — II.)

For 6 Persons.   *Time of Preparation:* 1½ hour.

3 oz. butter.	½ teaspoonful salt.
3 oz. flour.	4 tablespoonsful lemon juice.
3 oz. sugar.	A little grated lemon peel,
5 eggs.	¾ pint milk.

Melt the butter in a saucepan, mix the flour smoothly with the milk and add to the butter, stir well over the fire till of the consistency of a stiff paste. Then stand on one side. When cool, stir in the yolks, beaten up well with the sugar, the grated lemon peel and lemon juice and finally the whites, whisked stiffly.

Fill a well-buttered mould (*see* general directions: "Auflauf") and bake in a slow oven for f hour.

Mandel-Auflauf
(Almond Auflauf.)

To the Auflauf as in preceding recipe add 3 oz. of grated sweet almonds.

Kakao-Auflauf
(Cocoa Auflauf).

Prepare as Lemon Auflauf, substituting for the lemon juice and peel, 2 oz. cocoa and 2 extra oz. sugar and vanilla flavouring.

Auflauf von saurer Sahne
(Auflauf made with Sour Cream).

For 6 Persons.   *Time of Preparation:* 1½ hour.

5 eggs.	½ pint sour cream.
3 oz. flour.	½ teaspoonful salt.
4 oz. sugar.	Grated rind of ¼ lemon.

Beat the yolks well with the sugar and grated lemon peel, then stir in alternately the flour and sour cream and finally the stiffly-whisked whites of egg. Fill a well-buttered Auflauf mould (*see* general directions) and bake for ¾ hour.

This Auflauf may also be flavoured with grated almonds, or orange peel or vanilla.

Soufflé mit Aepfeln. — I.
(Soufflé with Apples.)

For 6 Persons.   *Time of Preparation:* 2 hours.

5 oz. sugar.	1 tablespoonful lemon juice.	6 eggs.
Grated rind	2 lbs. apples.	Grated rind of ½ lemon.

Bake the apples, then rub them through a hair sieve. Beat the eggs and sugar to a thick cream, then stir in the apple purée and the grated lemon peel, finally the whites, whisked very stiffly.

Fill a well-buttered mould (*see* general directions: "Auflauf") and bake for 30 minutes.

Fresh apricots or strawberries, passed through a sieve, may be substituted for the apples.

Anflauf yon Aepfeln.— II.
(Apple Auflauf.)

For 6 Persons.   *Time of Preparation:* ½ hour.

3 oz. butter.	3 oz. sugar.
6 eggs.	3 oz. grated roll.
2 lbs. apple purée.	

Cream the butter, add to it the yolks, well beaten with the sugar, and mix all well together. Add to this alternately the grated roll, apple purée and whisked whites of eggs, fill a well-buttered Auflauf mould (*see* general directions: "Auflauf") and bake 1 hour.

Kartoffel-Aaflauf
(Potato Soufflé.)

For 6 Persons.   *Time of Preparation:* 1 hour.

1 lb. boiled potatoes.	2 tablespoonsful lemon juice.
3 oz. sugar.	2 oz. grated sweet almonds.
3 oz. butter.	5 oz. grated bitter almonds
8 eggs.	A little grated lemon peel.
Salt.	

Cream the butter, add to it the yolks, beaten well with the sugar and the potatoes, rubbed through a sieve, grated almonds and lemon peel. When all is well mixed, fill a well-buttered Auflauf mould (*see* general directions: "Auflauf") and bake ¾ hour.

Auflauf von Apfelsinen
(Orange Auflauf.)

For 6 Persons.   *Time of Preparation:* 2 hours.

3 oz. butter,	Salt.	1 tablespoonful rum.
¾ pint milk.	3 oz. flour.	
6 eggs.	2 oranges.	

Melt the butter in a saucepan, mix the flour or milk smoothly, add them to the butter and heat, stirring continuously, to the consistency of dough. Stir in 2 beaten-up eggs and the juice of the oranges and stand on one side to cool. Beat the 6 yolks well with the sugar, add to them a tablespoonful of rum and half the peel of an orange, grated on lumps of sugar and stir into the cooled mixture, mixing well. Stir in finally the 6 whites, stiffly whisked. Fill a well-buttered Auflauf mould (*see* general directions: "Auflauf") and bake ¾ hour.

Nuss-Auflauf
(Nut Auflauf.)

For 6 Persons.   *Time of Preparation:* 1¼ hour.

6 eggs.	4 oz. hazelnut kernels.
6 oz. sugar.	1 tablespoonful rum.

Beat the sugar and yolks together well and stir in the finely-pounded nuts, and when well mixed, the stiffly-whisked whites of eggs.

Fill a well-buttered Auflauf mould (*see* general directions: "Auflauf") and bake ½ hour.

Semmel-Auflauf
(Roll Auflauf.)

For 6 Persons.   *Time of Preparation:* 1½ hour.

4 oz. breadcrumbs.	6 eggs.
3 oz. sugar.	4 bitter almonds or a little lemon
3 oz. butter.	juice.

Cream the butter, then stir in the beaten-up yolks and sugar and next the breadcrumbs and grated almonds. Mix well and finally stir in lightly the stiffly-whisked whites of eggs.

Fill a well-buttered Auflauf mould (see general directions: "Auflauf") and bake ¾ hour.

1 lb. stoned cherries, or 14 oz. thinly-sliced apples, sprinkled over with 5 oz. sugar may be substituted for the almond or lemon flavouring.

Gebackener Beis
(Baked Rice.)

For 6 Persons.   *Time of Preparation:* 2¼ hours.

¼ lb. rice.	1¼ pint milk.
3 oz. butter.	1 teaspoonful salt.
4 eggs.	6 bitter almonds.
2 oz. sugar.	Grated rind of 1 lemon.

Scald the rice and boil ¾ hour with the milk and butter till quite soft. Beat the yolks and sugar well together, and stir into the rice with the grated lemon peel and almonds. Then stir in lightly the whites, stiffly whisked, fill a well-buttered Auflauf mould (*see* general directions: "Auflauf") and bake ¾ hour.

Sprinkle over with sugar and serve with a fruit sauce. Sliced apples or jam may be substituted for the almond flavouring.

Griesspeise
(Semolina Auflauf.)

For 6 Persons.   *Time of Preparation:* 1½ hour.

2 oz. butter.	A little grated lemon	1 lb. semolina.
2 oz. sugar.	peel.	4 eggs,
2 oz. sweet almonds.	1¼ pint milk.	1 teaspoonful salt.

Boil the milk, semolina, butter and salt to the consistency of a stiff purée. Beat the yolks well with the sugar and add gradually with the grated almonds and lemon peel to the semolina, when the latter is cool, stirring in finally the whisked whites of eggs. Fill a well-buttered mould (Auflauf form, see general directions: "Auflauf") and bake in a slow oven for 1 hour.

An oz. of cocoa and an oz. of sugar may be added to this Auflauf, or 1 lb. sultanas and a tablespoonful of rum.

Puddinge
(*Puddings.*)

Puddings may be boiled in a well-floured cloth, but preferably in a special pudding basin or mould, with a tightly-fitting lid. Both the inside of the lid and of the mould itself should be well-buttered and then sprinkled over with breadcrumbs. The mould should not be more than ¾ full and should be stood in a saucepan of boiling water. The water should not come to the top of the mould, but fresh boiling water should be added from time to time to replace what boils away. Keep the lid of the saucepan on while the pudding is boiling. Puddings prepared according to the following recipes are always to be turned out and served with Fruchtor Weinschaum-Saucen. (*See* recipes.) Chocolate Pudding is served with Vanilla Sauce.

Reis-Pudding
(Rice Pudding.)

For 6 Persons.　　　　　*Time of Preparation:* 2½ hours.

4 oz. rice.	1¾ pint milk.	4 bitter almonds.
3 oz. butter.	3 oz. sugar.	A little grated lemon
5 eggs.	A pinch of carbonate of	peel.
1½ oz. sweet almonds,	soda.	1 teaspoonful salt.

Boil the rice in the milk for 1 hour with 1 teaspoonful salt, a pinch of carbonate of soda and 3 oz. butter. Then stir in 1 well-beaten up egg and stand on one side to cool.

Beat the 4 yolks with the sugar and add to them the grated almonds and a little lemon peel. Stir into the rice, alternately with the whites of eggs, whisked stiffly. Fill with this a well-buttered pudding basin, or mould, with a closely-fitting lid, and boil 1½ to 2 hours. (*See* general directions: "Puddings.")

Gries-Pudding
(Semolina Pudding.)

For 6 Persons.　　　　　*Time of Preparation:* 2½ hours.

1 pint milk.	4 oz. semolina.	A little grated lemon
3 oz. butter.	2 oz. sugar.	peel, or a few grated
6 eggs.	Salt.	bitter almonds.

Put on the milk with the salt and butter, shake into it the semolina, stirring continuously and boil to the consistency of a fairly thick purée. Then remove from the fire and stir into it 1 well-beaten eggs.

Beat the 5 yolks well with the sugar and flavour with a little grated lemon peel or bitter almonds, as preferred. Stir, alternately, with the whites of eggs whisked stiffly, into the semolina.

Fill with this a well-buttered pudding basin, or mould, with a closely-fitting lid and boil 1½ hour. (*See* general directions: "Puddings.")

Serve with Fruchtor Wein-Sauce. (*See* recipes.)

Nuss-Pudding
(Nut Pudding.)

For 6 Persons.   *Time of Preparation:* 2 hours.

½ lb. hazelnut kernels,	2 ground cloves.	1 tablespoonful rum.
1½ oz. grated roll.	Vanilla to flavour.	1½ oz. chopped can-
1 teaspoonful ground	½ lb. sugar.	died peel.
cinnamon.	6 eggs.	

Beat the yolks and sugar for ½ hour, then stir in all ingredients adding last the nuts, finely chopped or passed through the mincing machine, and the whites of eggs, whisked stiffly.

Fill with this a well-buttered pudding basin, or mould, with a closely-fitting lid, and boil 1¼ hour. (See general directions: "Puddings.")

Serve with Weinschaum-Sauce. (*See* recipe.)

Schokoladen-Pudding
(Chocolate Pudding.)

For 6 Persons.   *Time of Preparation:* 2½ hours.

4 oz. flour.	4 eggs.	4 oz. sugar.
2 oz. butter.	4 oz. chocolate.	½ pint milk.

Melt the butter in a saucepan. Mix the chocolate and flour smoothly in the milk, beat it up and pour it into the butter, stirring continuously till of the consistency of a thick purée. Then remove from the fire and stir into it, when a little cooled, the yolks, well beaten with the sugar and finally the whites of eggs, whisked stiffly. Fill with this a well-buttered pudding basin, or mould, with a closely-fitting lid, and boil 1½ hour. (*See* general directions: "Puddings.")

Serve with Vanilla Sauce. (*See* recipe.)

Kakao-Pudding
(Cocoa Pudding.)

For 6 Persons.   *Time of Preparation*: 2½ hours.

½ pint milk.	4 eggs.	1 teaspoonful cinna-
2 oz. cocoa.	2 oz. butter.	mon or vanilla.
4 oz. flour.	6 oz. sugar.	

Melt the butter in a saucepan. Mix the flour smoothly in the milk, beat it up, pour into the butter and heat, stirring continuously, till it becomes a thick paste. Then remove from the fire, and, while warm, stir in the cocoa. When cooler, stir in the yolks, well beaten with sugar and finally the whites of eggs, whisked stiffly. Fill with this a well-buttered pudding basin, or mould, with a closely-fitting lid, and boil 1½ hour. (*See* general directions: "Puddings.")

Serve with Vanilla or Almond Sauce. (*See* recipes.)

Mandel-Padding
(Almond Pudding.)

For 6 Persons.   *Time of Preparation:* 2½ hours.

4 oz. flour.	1 pint milk.	4 oz. sweet almonds.
4 oz. sugar.	4 oz. butter.	6 eggs.

Melt the butter in a saucepan. Mix the flour smoothly in the milk, beat it up, pour it into the butter and heat, stirring continuously, till somewhat thick. Then remove from the fire, stir in the 6 yolks, well beaten with the sugar, the grated almonds and finally the 6 whites of eggs, whisked stiffly.

Fill with this a well-buttered pudding basin, or mould, with a closely-fitting lid, and boil 1½ hour. (*See* general directions: "Puddings.")

Nudel-Pudding

For 6 Persons.   *Time of Preparation:* 2 hours

¾ pint milk.	6 eggs.	A little grated lemon
2 oz. butter.	4 oz. finely-cut Nudeln.	peel.
1 oz. sweet almonds.	3 oz. sugar.	

Boil the milk with the butter and salt, then strew in the Nudeln, using either some made according to recipe, or those obtainable at most German Delikatessen shops. Boil to a fairly firm purée, then stir in 2 well-beaten eggs. Beat the 4 yolks well with the sugar, and add, with the grated almonds and lemon peel, stirring in finally the 4 whites of eggs, whisked stiffly.

Fill with this a well-buttered pudding basin, or mould, with closely-fitting lid and boil 1¼ hour. (*See* general directions ("Puddings.")

This pudding may be varied by the addition of 4 oz. sultanas, or ½ lb. boiled stoned prunes, or 5 oz. thinly-sliced apples.

Kartoffel-Pudding
(Potato Pudding.)

For 6 Persons.   *Time of Preparation:* 2½ hours.

½ lb. boiled potatoes.	3 oz. butter.	15 bitter almonds.
3 oz. almonds.	3 oz. sugar.	4 eggs.

Cream the butter, add to it the sugar, beaten well with the yolks and stir well for 15 minutes. Then add the grated almonds, half the quantity of the potatoes (which should be dry and floury and be rubbed through a sieve) and half the whites of eggs, whisked very stiffly. Mix well, then stir in the remainder of the potatoes and whisked whites of eggs.

Fill a well-buttered pudding basin or mould, with closely-fitting lid and boil 1½ hour. (*See* general directions: "Puddings.")

Serve with a wine sauce.

Kartoffelmehl-Pudding
(Potato Flour Pudding.)

For 6 Persons. *Time of Preparation:* 2½ hours.

4 oz. potato flour.	6 eggs.
3 oz. butter.	½ teaspoonful salt.
4 oz. sugar.	2 tablespoonsful lemon juice.
¾ pint milk.	The grated rind of 1 lemon.

Melt the butter in a saucepan. Mix the flour smoothly in the milk, beat it up and pour into the butter. Add the salt and stir continuously, till of the consistency of a thick purée. Then remove from the fire and stir in at once 2 beaten-up eggs. Beat 4 yolks well with the sugar, add to the mixture when a little cooled, with the grated lemon peel and lemon juice and finally stir in the 4 whites of eggs, whisked stiffly.

Fill with this a well-buttered basin, or mould, with a closely-fitting lid, and boil 1½ hour. (*See* general directions: "Puddings.")

Semmel-Pudding
(Bread Pudding.)

For 6 Persons. *Time of Preparation:* 2½ to 3 hours.

4 oz. bread, cut into dice.	1 teaspoonful salt.	3 oz. butter.
¾ pint milk.	10 bitter almonds	6 eggs.
	4 oz. currants.	

Soak the bread in the milk. Cream the butter, beat the yolks well and mix thoroughly the butter, yolks, grated almonds, sugar and soaked bread, stirring in lastly the currants and whites of eggs, whisked stiffly.

Fill with this a well-buttered basin, or mould, with a closely-fitting lid, and boil 2 hours. (*See* general directions: "Puddings.")

This pudding may be improved by the addition of a tablespoonful of rum and of lemon juice and 3 oz. chopped candied peel.

Pumpernickel-Pudding.— I.

For 6 Persons.   *Time of Preparation:* 1½ hour.

4 oz. grated Pumpernickel.
4 oz. chopped candied peel.
4 ground cloves.
4 oz. sweet almonds.
4 oz. currants.

6 eggs.
A little grated lemon peel.
8 oz. sugar.
1 teaspoonful ground cinnamon.
½ pint red wine.

Beat the yolks well with 4 oz. sugar and stir in the whites of eggs, whisked stiffly, and the cinnamon, cloves and -lemon peel. Then add the grated Pumpernickel, finely-chopped candied peel and almonds, and the currants. Mix thoroughly and fill a well-buttered pudding basin, or mould, with closely-fitting lid, and boil 1 hour. (*See* general directions: "Puddings.")

Turn out and serve hot, pouring over it the wine which has been boiled up with 4 oz. sugar. This pudding tastes excellent served cold, with whipped cream.

Pumpernickel-Pudding.— II.

| 4 oz. chocolate. | 4 oz. grated Pumpernickel. | 4 oz. butter. 4 oz. sugar. | 4 eggs. |

Melt the butter and stir into it the grated Pumpernickel and the chocolate. Mix thoroughly and then add the 4 yolks, beaten well with 4 oz. sugar and finally the 4 whites of eggs whisked stiffly.

Fill with this a well-buttered pudding basin, or mould, with closely-fitting lid and boil 1½ hour. (*See* general directions: "Puddings.")

This pudding is also excellent served cold, with whipped cream.

Flammeri

(*Flummery.*)

Feiner Flammeri

(Cornflour Flummery.)

For 6 Persons.   *Time of Preparation:* ½ hour.

1 pint boiling milk.
1 gill cold milk.
2 oz. sugar.
Vanilla flavouring.

1 oz. fresh butter.
2 oz. cornflour.
4 eggs.
½ teaspoonful salt.

Boil up the butter, sugar and salt with the pint of milk and add vanilla flavouring. Mix the cornflour smoothly with the gill of cold milk, beat up with the yolks and add to the boiling milk. Boil up together, stirring continuously, and then stir in at once the whites of eggs, whisked stiffly. Pour into a mould that has been rinsed in cold water and turn out when cold. Serve with a cold Weinschaum-Sauce or Frucht-Sauce. (*See* recipes.)

Gries-Flammeri
(Semolina Flummery.)

For 6 Persons.   *Time of Preparation:* 1 hour.

1½ pints milk.	6 eggs.
4 oz. semolina.	4 tablespoonsful cold milk.
1 teaspoonful salt.	Vanilla *or* lemon flavouring.
3 oz. sugar.	

Boil the milk, adding the flavouring desired, then strew in the semolina, stirring well, and boil 15 minutes. Beat the yolks with 4 tablespoonsful cold milk, stir into the semolina and bring to the boil again. Then add at once the stiffly-whisked whites of eggs. Pour into a mould, rinsed with cold water, and turn out when cold.

Flammeri von Reis
(Rice Flummery.)

For 6 Persons.   *Time of Preparation:* 2 hours.

8 oz. rice.	½ lb. ratifias.	1 teaspoonful salt.
1 oz. butter.	1 quart milk.	
10 bitter almonds.	3 oz. sugar.	

Scald the rice twice and boil in the milk for an hour till soft. Then add salt, sugar and butter and the grated almonds. Rinse a mould with cold water, line it with ratifia biscuits and pour in the rice. When cold, turn out and serve with Frucht-Sauce. (*See* recipe.)

Mehl-Flammeri
(Flour Flummery.)

For 6 Persons.   *Time of Preparation:* 1 hour.

1 quart milk, boiled.	¼ lb. sugar.	Vanilla *or* almond
4 eggs.	6 oz. flour.	flavouring.
½ pint cold milk.	A little lemon juice.	
½ teaspoonful salt.	A dash of Maraschino.	

Bring a quart of milk to the boil with a little salt. Add the sugar and flavourings. Mix the flour smoothly with a little of the ½ pint of cold milk and add to the 4 eggs, well beaten with the rest of the cold milk, and a little salt. Add this to the boiling milk and boil for a further 3 minutes, pour into a mould that has been rinsed with cold water and turn out when cold.

Zitronen-Flammeri
(Lemon Flummery.)

1½ pint water.	4 eggs.
6 tablespoonsful lemon juice.	¾ lb. sugar.
The thinly-peeled rind of ½ lemon.	4 oz. sifted flour.
½ pint cider.	½ teaspoonful salt.

Boil the thinly-peeled rind of ½ lemon in 1½ pint water for 2 minutes, then take it out. Mix the flour smoothly in the cider and beat it up with the yolks, sugar, lemon juice and salt. Add to the boiling water and boil 3 minutes. Then draw on one side and stir in the whites of eggs, whisked stiffly. Pour into a mould that has been rinsed with cold water. When cold, turn out and serve with Fruchtor Wein-Sauce. (*See* recipes.)

Apfel-Flammeri
(Apple Flummery.)

For 6 Persons.   *Time of Preparation:* 1 hour.

1½ lb. apples.	A few drops of cochineal.
1½ pint water.	A small piece of lemon peel.
¼ lb. sugar.	A little cinnamon.
2 leaves of gelatine	3 oz. sifted flour.

Peel and slice the apples and put them on in a pint of water. When they are soft, rub them through a sieve and boil them up again with sugar, 2 leaves of gelatine, the lemon juice, lemon peel and cinnamon. Add the flour, smoothly mixed in ½ pint water, colour with a few drops of cochineal and boil for a few minutes longer. Pour into a mould that has been rinsed with cold water, and when cold, turn out and serve with whipped cream.

Flammeri mit Schokolade
(Chocolate Flummery.)

For 6 Persons.   *Time of Preparation*: 1 hour.

1¾ pint milk.	1 teaspoonful salt.	2 oz. sugar.
4 oz. chocolate.	4 oz. semolina.	

Strew the semolina in the boiling milk, then gradually the salt, sugar and grated chocolate. Boil to the consistency of a thick purée and pour into a mould that has been rinsed with cold water. When cold, turn out and serve with Vanilla Sauce. (*See* recipe.)

Semmel-Flammeri
(Roll Flummery.)

For 6 Persons.   *Time of Preparation:* 1½ hour.

4 oz. grated roll.	2 tablespoonsful rum.	A little lemon peel.
1 pint water.	1 tablespoonful lemon	4 oz. sugar.
A pinch of salt.	juice.	

Soak the grated roll for an hour in the milk, boil 5 minutes with the lemon peel and then pass through a hair sieve. Stir in the sugar, lemon juice, rum and salt, mix well and pour into a mould that has been rinsed with cold water. When cold, turn out and serve with Frucht-Sauce. (*See* recipe.)

This should be prepared a day before required, so that it may thoroughly set.

Flammeri mit Eiweiss
(Flummery with White of Egg.)

For 6 Persons.   *Time of Preparation:* 1 hour.

4 oz. potato flour.	A small piece of closely pared orange
6 whites of eggs.	peel.
1 quart boiling milk.	2 oz. grated sweet almonds.
½ pint cold milk.	½ teaspoonful salt.

Into the boiling milk put the sugar, salt, grated almonds and the orange peel. Add the cold milk, with which the flour has been smoothly mixed, and boil 2 minutes, stirring continuously. Then stir in at once the whites of eggs, whisked stiffly, and pour into a mould that has been rinsed in cold water. Turn out when cold.

Rote Grütze

2 lbs. of fruit.	Ground rice, sago or corn-flour.
¼ lb. loaf sugar.	1 pint water.

Put half a pound each of red and black currants, cherries and raspberries into a pan, add 1 pint of water and a quarter of a pound of loaf sugar.

Stew gently until soft, then strain off the juice through a hair sieve and measure it. Put the juice on to boil. To each pint of juice allow 2 large tablespoonsful of ground rice, mixing latter smoothly with cold water. When the juice boils, pour in the rice. Let it come to the boil.

Pour the mixture into a mould which has been rinsed out with cold water. When cold, turn out. Serve with cream or custard.

Sago or cornflour may be used instead of ground rice, and bottled syrup instead of the fresh fruit.

Cremes

(Creams.)

Vanillen-Creme
(Vanilla Cream.)

For 6 Persons.   *Time of Preparation:* 2 hours.

1 pint milk.	6 eggs.	5 leaves of gelatine.
3 oz. sugar.	1 vanilla bean.	

Beat the yolks and sugar well together. Boil up ½ pint of the milk with the vanilla and a pinch of carbonate of soda. Beat the remaining milk with the yolks and sugar and add to the boiling milk, boiling up again and stirring continuously. Add the dissolved gelatine, pour into a basin, stand in a cool place and stir until it begins to thicken. Then stir in the whites of eggs, whisked stiffly. Pour into a glass dish and decorate with little heaps of stewed or preserved fruit, or jelly.

Sultan-Creme
(Sultana Cream.)

Prepared according to preceding recipe; 4 oz. of sultanas, boiled with sugar and then dried, and 2 oz. finely-chopped candied peel are stirred into the cream just before the whisked whites of eggs.

Mandel-Creme
(Almond Cream.)

Prepared like Vanilla Cream, but 8 bitter almonds and 2 oz. sweet almonds, grated finely, are substituted for the vanilla.

Nuss-Creme
(Nut Cream.)

For 6 Persons.   *Time of Preparation:* 1 hour.

1¼ pint milk.	1 tablespoonful sifted flour.
4 oz. hazelnut kernels.	3 eggs.
4 oz. sugar.	5 leaves of gelatine.

Scald the nut kernels, scrape the skins off and pound finely. Put on half of the milk to boil with the sugar. Beat the yolks with the remainder of the milk, add to the boiling milk and boil up again, adding the dissolved gelatine and a pinch of salt. Pour into a basin, stand in a cool place and stir until it begins to thicken. Then stir in the stiffly-whisked whites of eggs and the pounded nuts. Pour into a glass dish and garnish with nuts.

Sohokoladen-Creme. — I.
(Chocolate Cream.)

For 6 Persons.   *Time of Preparation:* 2 hours.

½ pint milk.	4 oz. grated chocolate.
½ oz. cocoa.	3 oz. sugar.
6 whites of eggs, *or* ½ pint whipped	5 leaves of gelatine (8 leaves, if the
cream.	cream is to be turned out).

Boil the milk, then stir in the sugar, cocoa, half the grated chocolate and the dissolved gelatine. Pour into a basin, stand in a cool place and stir until it begins to thicken. Then stir in the whipped cream, or whites of eggs, whisked stiffly, sprinkled over with the remaining chocolate. Pour into a glass dish and serve with or without a thick vanilla sauce. (See recipe, page 67.)

Sohokoladen-Creme. — II.
(Chocolate Cream without Eggs.)

¾ pint milk.	1 oz. sugar.
1 oz. potato flour.	4 oz. chocolate.

Boil up half the milk. Mix the chocolate and flour smoothly in the remaining cold milk, add to the boiling milk, boil up together and pour into a dish. When cold, decorate with ratilia biscuits or whipped cream.

Schokoladen-Creme auf kaltem Wege zubereitet
(Chocolate Cream prepared without cooking.)

¼ lb. chocolate.	6 leaves of gelatine.
1 tablespoonful cocoa.	½ pint whipped cream.
Vanilla flavouring.	Whites of 4 eggs.
½ pint water.	

Grate the chocolate and mix it with the cocoa and half of the water. Dissolve the gelatine in the remaining water, warmed, and stir it into the chocolate, continuing stirring until the gelatine is quite cool again. Then add the vanilla flavouring, a little sugar, if desired, the whipped cream and the stiffly-whisked whites of eggs. Fill a mould that has been oiled and stand in a cool place for 5 hours.

Serve turned out, the dish decorated with little heaps of whipped cream. The mould may also be lined with ratifia or other small biscuits.

Rumspeise
(Rum Cream.)

1 quart milk.	1 oz. sifted flour.	¾ oz. gelatine.
1 gill rum.	4 oz. sugar,	A little cochineal.

Boil 1½ pint milk with the sugar. Mix the sifted flour smoothly in ½ pint of cold milk and add to the boiling milk with the dissolved gelatine. Stand on one side to cool, and when the cream begins to set, stir in the rum and colour with a little cochineal. Pour into a mould rinsed with cold water and when set, serve turned out, with Vanilla Sauce or whipped cream.

Russische Creme
(Russian Cream.)

8 oz. sugar.	½ gill orange juice.
4 eggs.	2 tablespoonsful lemon juice.
10 leaves of gelatine.	½ pint white wine.
½ pint whipped cream.	½ gill rum.

Beat the sugar, orange juice, eggs, wine and rum well together. Stir in a saucepan till it thickens, then add the dissolved gelatine. Remove from the fire, whisk briskly and stir in the whites of eggs beaten to a snow. Pour into a mould rinsed with cold water, and, when set, turn out.

Kaffee-Creme
(Coffee Cream.)

1¼ pint milk.	2 oz. sifted flour.
2 oz. coarsely-ground coffee.	4 oz. sugar.
4 eggs.	

Boil up ½ pint milk with the coffee and strain through a hair sieve. When cold, stir in the flour and yolks beaten smoothly together. Then add the remaining milk, bring all to the boil, and finally stir in the stiffly-whisked whites of eggs. Pour into a dish and serve cold.

Zitronen-Creme
(Lemon Cream.)

½ lb. sugar.
4 leaves of gelatine.

6 tablespoonsful lemon juice.
6 eggs.

Beat the yolks well with the sugar, and add the gelatine that has been dissolved in the warmed lemon juice. Then stir in the stiffly-whisked whites of eggs and pour into a glass dish.

A chocolate cream may be prepared in this way, 3 oz. grated chocolate being substituted for the lemon juice.

Apfelsinen-Creme
(Orange Cream.)

½ lb. sugar.
5 leaves of gelatine.
1 gill orange juice.

2 tablespoonsful lemon juice.
6 eggs.

Prepare in the same manner as Lemon Cream.

Ponsch-Creme
(Punch Cream.)

4 eggs.
8 leaves of gelatine.
1 gill rum.

½ pint white wine.
10 oz. sugar.

3 tablespoonsful lemon juice.

Warm the wine and dissolve the gelatine in it, then stand on one side. Beat the yolks and sugar well together, stir in the rum and lemon juice into the half-set wine jelly, and lastly the stiffly-whisked whites of eggs. Pour into a glass dish, decorating, when set, with ratifias.

Wein-Creme
(Wine Cream.)

½ pint white wine.
4 eggs.
3 tablespoonsful lemon juice.

4 oz. sugar.
2 leaves of gelatine.

Beat the eggs with the wine, lemon juice and sugar, add the gelatine, dissolved, and bring just to the boil. When cool, pour into a glass dish and when set, decorate with little heaps of fruit jelly.

Schlagsahne

(Dishes Prepared from Whipped Cream.)

Schlagsahne mit Pumpernickel
(Whipped Cream with Pumpernickel.)

1 pint whipped cream.	4 oz. sugar.
Vanilla flavouring.	4 oz. grated Pumpernickel.

Mix the sugar and the grated Pumpernickel, place half the quantity in the bottom of a glass dish, and on it, the whipped cream flavoured with vanilla, then on this, the remaining Pumpernickel as a top layer. The Pumpernickel may also be mixed with 4 oz. chocolate, the sugar being then omitted.

Or, pounded ratifia biscuits may be mixed with the Pumpernickel, and coffee extract added to the cream. An excellent variation of this dish is to place on the lower layer of Pumpernickel, fresh fruit, such as strawberries, raspberries, or currants, well sprinkled over with castor sugar.

Schlagsahne zum Stürzen
(Whipped Cream in a Mould.)

¾ pint whipped cream.	4 oz. sugar.
½ gill water.	A little vanilla flavouring.
6 leaves of gelatine.	

Dissolve the gelatine in the water and stir it into the whipped cream with the sugar and a little vanilla flavouring. Whisk all together and fill a mould that has first been rinsed with cold water. When set, turn out and serve with strawberries, red currants, or preserves.

Tutti Frutti mit Schlagsahne
(Fruit with Whipped Cream.)

1 pint various fruits.	4 leaves of gelatin dissolved in 2 ta-
4 oz. ratifia biscuits.	blespoonsful water.
1 pint cream.	

Line a glass dish with little ratifia biscuits. Then place alternate layers of cream (in which the dissolved gelatine has been stirred) and of various kinds of fruit, stewed or preserved, the topmost layer being of whipped cream.

Königin Reisspeise — Himmelspeise
(Rice à la Reine.)

4 oz. best rice.	12 leaves of gelatine (1 oz.).	1 vanilla bean.
1½ pint cream.	4 oz. sugar.	2 tablespoonsful water.
¾ pint whipped cream.		3 tablespoonsful rum.

Scald the rice 4 times, the fourth time with carbonate of soda in the water. Then boil it in the cream with a pinch of salt and the vanilla, adding 4 leaves of gelatine, dissolved in a little boiling water, and the sugar. Stand the rice on one side to cool, stirring occasionally. Dissolve the remaining 8 leaves of gelatine in 2 tablespoonsful boiling water. Add it, with 3 tablespoonsful rum, to the cream, whisked very stiffly, and then stir into the rice. Rinse a mould with cold water, fill it with the rice cream, stand it for at least 2 hours in a cool place, then turn out and serve with fruit syrup.

Schlagsahne mit Kaffee
(Coffee Whipped Cream.)

¾ pint cream.
Half a vanilla stick pounded with a little sugar.
8 leaves of gelatine dissolved in a gill of strong coffee.
4 oz. sugar.

Dissolve the gelatine and stir it into the coffee and whipped cream, adding the sugar and vanilla. Pour into a mould, rinsed with cold water, and turn out when set.

Schlagsahne mit Schokolade
(Chocolate Whipped Cream.)

¾ pint cream.	8 leaves of gelatine (½ oz.).	3 oz. sugar.
4 oz. chocolate.		½ gill water.

Dissolve the gelatine in the water and stir it into the other ingredients. Prepare as in preceding recipe.

Schlagsahne mit Nüssen
(Nut Whipped Cream.)

¾ pint cream.	4 oz. hazelnut kernels *or* grated almonds.
8 leaves of gelatine (½ oz.).	4 oz. sugar.
½ gill water.	

Prepare as preceding recipes.

Schlagsahne mit Apfelsinen
(Orange Whipped Cream.)

¾ pint cream.	5 oz. sugar.
1 gill orange juice.	2 tablespoonsful lemon juice.
Orange peel rubbed on sugar.	8 leaves of gelatine (½ oz.).

Dissolve the gelatine in the orange juice and prepare as the preceding recipes.

Schlagsahne mit Früchten
(Whipped Cream with various Fruits.)

¾ pint cream.	1 gill fruit syrup.
10 leaves of gelatine.	1 gill finely-chopped fruits.

Cut up various kinds of fruit, such as strawberries, pineapple, peaches, apricots, etc., into small pieces. Dissolve the gelatine in the fruit syrup and whisk it with the cream. Rinse a mould with cold water and fill it with alternate layers of the cream and fruit. When set, turn out.

Sonstige Susse Speisen
(*Other Sweets.*)

Zitronenreis
(Lemon Rice.)

½ lb. rice.	4 tablespoonsful lemon juice.
1 oz. butter.	Grated rind of 2 lemons.
1 quart water.	Salt and sugar to taste.

Scald the rice and boil it with the butter and a little salt. Add the grated rind of 2 lemons, 4 tablespoonsful lemon juice and sugar to taste.

Milchreis
(Rice with Milk.)

For 6 Persons.	*Time of Preparation:* 1¾ hour.

½ lb. rice.	1 quart milk.
Vanilla, lemon *or* bitter almond flavouring.	A little salt.

Scald the rice 3 times, the third time adding a pinch of carbonate of soda to the boiling water. Drain well and then throw into the boiling milk; add whatever flavouring is desired and boil up. Then cover and draw on one side, simmering gently until the rice is soft. Shake the saucepan occasionally.

The flavouring may be omitted and the rice served with a sprinkling of sugar and cinnamon.

Apfelreis
(Apple Rice.)

For 6 Persons.   *Time of Preparation:* 1½ hour.

½ lb. rice.	1½ pint water.	2 lbs. apples.
1 tablespoonful salt.	2 oz. butter.	
2 oz. sugar.	A piece of lemon peel.	

Scald the rice twice. Peel the apples, cut them into dice and fill a buttered pudding basin (that is provided with closely-fitting lid) with alternate layers of apples and rice, the top and bottom layer consisting of apples. Boil up the water with the butter, sugar and salt, and pour it over. Then place the lid on the mould and boil for 2 hours.

Turn out the rice on to a deep dish and serve sprinkled over with sugar.

Stoned cherries may be substituted for apples.

Weinreis
(Wine Rice.)

For 6 Persons.   *Time of Preparation:* 2 hours.

| ¼ lb. rice. | 5 oz. sugar. |
| 4 tablespoonsful lemon juice. | ¾ pint white wine. |

Put on the rice in cold water, pour off the water as soon as it boils and replace by fresh cold water. Repeat this several times, then drain the rice on a sieve. Boil up ½ pint of the wine with the sugar and lemon juice, shake the rice into it and boil it till the grains are soft. Let the rice cool a little and then stir in the remaining wine. Serve in a glass dish, ornamented with little heaps of various bottled fruits.

Himbeerschaum
(Raspberry Froth.)

| 3 whites of eggs. | 3 oz. castor sugar. |
| 4 oz. jam (currant, raspberry *or* cranberry). | |

Whisk all together for 1 hour and serve in a glass dish.

Apfelschnee
(Apple Snow.)

1 lb. stiff apple purée.

3 oz. sugar.

6 whites of eggs.

2 tablespoonsful lemon juice.

Whisk the whites very stiffly, then stir in the sugar, lemon juice, and finally the apple purée. Serve in a glass dish, garnished with jelly.

Schaumspeise
(Sponge.)

¾ pint fruit syrup.

8 whites of eggs.

¾ pint cider *or* water.

3 oz. sifted flour.

Sugar to taste.

Boil the syrup with the sugar and wine and add the flour, mixed smoothly in a little water. When this has boiled a few minutes, remove from the fire and stir into it the stiffly-whisked whites of eggs. Fill a mould that has been rinsed with cold water and turn out when cold. Serve with Vanilla Sauce (*see* recipe) or whipped cream.

Arme Ritter
(Poor Knight's Pudding.)

Time of Preparation: 1 hour.

18 slices Vienna bread.

¾ pint milk.

1 teaspoonful salt.

2 oz. grated roll.

4 oz. butter.

8 bitter almonds.

3 eggs.

Beat up together the milk, eggs, salt and grated almonds and pour over the slices of bread, so that they are well soaked through. Then sprinkle over with grated roll and fry a pale brown on both sides in butter. Serve with Fruit Sauce, etc.

Karthäuser Klösse
(Carthusian Fritters.)

For 6 Persons.   *Time of Preparation:* 1½ hour.

9 long rolls.

4 eggs.

5 bitter almonds.

1 pint milk.

1 teaspoonful salt.

2 oz. sugar.

Grate off the outer crust of the rolls. Cut the rolls in halves lengthwise and pour over them the milk which has been well beaten with the eggs and other ingredients. When thoroughly soaked, sprinkle in the grated roll and fry in plenty of butter or fat. Sprinkle over with castor sugar and cinnamon and serve with Fruit Sauce. They may be further decorated with sweet almonds, cut into thin strips; in this case, serve with Wine Sauce.

Kaiser-Schmarren

For 6 Persons.   *Time of Preparation: ½ hour.*

6 eggs.	5 oz. flour.
1 pint cream.	1 teaspoonful salt.
4 oz. currants.	Grated peel of half a lemon.
4 oz. butter.	4 oz. grated sweet almonds.

Mix all the ingredients, except the butter, into a dough. Fry this brown on both sides in the butter. Then pull, or cut, into smaller pieces and fry each crisply. Serve on a hot dish and sprinkle over with sugar.

Tiroler Strudel

For 6 Persons.   *Time of Preparation: 3½ hours.*

½ lb. flour.	3 oz. butter.	2 oz. grated sweet almonds.
1 gill milk.	8 yolks of eggs.	
4 oz. sugar.	4 whites of eggs.	½ teaspoonful salt.
1 oz. yeast.		½ pint cream.

Cream 2 oz. of the butter and add 4 yolks to it. Then stir in the flour and the yeast, dissolved in a gill of lukewarm water. Mix thoroughly. Place the dough on a board, well dredged with flour, roll out to less than ¼ inch in thickness and spread with the following mixture: 4 yolks, beaten with 4 oz. sugar, and then the 4 whites, whisked stiffly, stirred into them with 2 oz. grated almonds.

Roll together and then curl round on itself (in snaillike form) and place to rise in a pan thickly buttered with an oz. of butter. When well risen, bake in a hot oven. After the first 10 minutes, pour over the Strudel 1 pint of cream and bake for a further 30 minutes.

Mandelbrei
(Almond Shape.)

1 pint milk.	10 eggs.
½ lb. sugar.	60 finely-pounded sweet almonds.
10 oz. potato flour.	15 finely-pounded bitter almonds.

Stir into a pint of milk ½ lb. sugar, 10 oz. potato flour, 60 finely-pounded sweet almonds and 15 bitter ones. Boil to a thick pulp, stirring continuously.

153

Then beat 10 eggs to a froth, and add to the pulp, simmering some minutes longer. Rinse a mould with cold water, pour in the mixture and serve with Vanilla Sauce. (*See* recipe.)

Kompott
(*Compôte.*)

Rhabarber-Kompott
(Rhubarb Compôte.)

1 lb. rhubarb.	2 tablespoonsful lemon juice.
1 gill water.	½ lb. sugar.
Cinnamon *or* lemon peel	1 leaf of gelatine.
A drop or two of cochineal.	

Peel the rhubarb and cut into short lengths. Boil a piece of cinnamon stick or lemon peel in the water for 5 minutes. Then put in the rhubarb, removing the flavouring, and boil lo minutes. Add the lemon juice, the dissolved gelatine and a few drops of cochineal.

Stachelbeer-Kompott
(Gooseberry Compôte.)

1 lb. gooseberries.	1 gill water.
A small piece of cinnamon stick.	½ lb. sugar.
A pinch of carbonate of soda.	

Top and tail the gooseberries and throw them into a quart of boiling water with a pinch of carbonate of soda. As soon as the fruit rises to the surface, take it out and drain on a sieve, dashing a little cold water over it.

Boil the sugar with the cinnamon in a gill of water for 5 minutes, then put the gooseberries in and bring once more just to the boil. Take out, boil the syrup down a little and pour over the gooseberries.

Himbeer-Kompott
(Raspberry Compôte.)

1 lb. raspberries.	1 gill water.
A pinch of potato flour.	10 oz. sugar.

Boil up the sugar and the water and pour over the fruit. Leave standing for 15 minutes. Then strain off the syrup, boil it for 5 minutes, thicken with potato flour, and pour over the fruit again.

Johannisbeer-Kompott
(Red Currant Compôte.)

1 lb. currants.

A pinch of potato flour.

14 oz. sugar.

½ gill water.

Prepare as Raspberry Compôte.

Apfel-Kompott
(Apple Compôte.)

1 lb. peeled apples.

2 tablespoonsful lemon juice.

8 oz. sugar.

½ pint water.

Boil up the water and sugar, add the lemon juice and the apples, cut into thick slices, and shake to and fro over the fire, keeping the saucepan covered till the apples are transparent. Then take out, boil the syrup down and pour over them.

Apfelmus
(Apple Fool.)

2 lbs. apples.

5 oz. sugar.

Peel and core the apples, cutting them up and putting them into cold water at once to preserve the colour. Then place in a saucepan with 3 table-spoonsful of water, keeping the lid on and shaking the pan to and fro frequently. When the apples are soft, rub them through a hair sieve and sweeten with sugar. A flavouring of cinnamon or lemon may be added if desired.

Pflaumen-Kompott
(Plum Compôte.)

1 lb. plums.

A piece of cinnamon stick.

½ lb. sugar.

½ gill water.

Boil the water with the sugar, put in the plums, washed and stoned, boil up once, then take out and drain. Let the juice boil down to a thick syrup and pour it over the plums.

Mirabellen, greengages, etc., are prepared in the same way.

Birnen-Kompott
(Pear Compôte.)

2 lbs. pears,

¾ pint water.

A little lemon peel.

A pinch of potato flour.

3 oz. sugar.

2 tablespoonsful lemon | juice.

Peel, core and halve the pears. Boil up the water with sugar and lemon peel. Then put in the pears and lemon juice and stew gently with the lid on the saucepan. When soft, take out the pears, thicken the syrup with a little potato flour and pour over them.

Kirschen-Kompott
(Cherry Compôte.)

1 lb. Morella cherries.	10 oz. sugar.
A piece of cinnamon stick.	

Wash and stone the cherries, sprinkle the sugar over them and leave them to stand for 15 minutes. Then pour off the syrup and boil up with the cinnamon. Add the cherries and boil for 2 minutes, shaking the saucepan continually.
Should sweet cherries be taken, add a little lemon juice and allow less sugar.

Heidelbeer-Kompott
(Bilberry Compôte.)

1 lb. bilberries.	3 oz. sugar.
A piece of cinnamon stick.	A pinch of potato flour.

Pick over and wash the bilberries and drain them on a sieve. Then mix well with the sugar, put in a saucepan and boil for 5 minutes with a little cinnamon, thickening with a pinch of potato flour. It is an improvement to add a few raspberries or red currants.

Preisselbeer-Kompott
(Cranberry Compôte.)

Prepare as Bilberry Compôte, but with considerably more sugar. The addition of a few raspberries or blackberries is a great improvement.

Backpflaumen-Kompott
(Compôte of Prunes.)

½ lb. prunes.	2 cloves.	2 oz. loaf sugar.
Rind of a lemon.	¼ pint wine.	
¼ pint water.	Angelica.	

Put half a pound of prunes into a stewpan with 1 pint water and ¼ pint wine (Marsala will do), the rind of half a lemon pared very thinly, 2 cloves and 2 oz. loaf sugar.

Simmer very gently till the fruit is quite tender. Let it get cold, take out the lemon and cloves, and add a few diamond-shaped pieces of angelica. It is then ready for use.

Gefrorenes

(Ices.)

Vanillen-Eis.— I.
(Vanilla Ice. — I.)

1 pint milk.	2 extra yolks.	Half a vanilla stick.
2 eggs.	6 oz. sugar.	

Bring ¾ pint of the milk slowly to the boil with the vanilla stick. In the meantime, beat up the 4 yolks and the 2 whites with the sugar and put them in a saucepan, not directly over the fire. Pour in the remaining ¼ pint of cold milk and the boiling vanilla-flavoured milk and beat all up together continuously till the liquid becomes of the consistency of thick cream. Then pour into a basin and continue stirring till cold. Freeze in a freezing machine. Directions are supplied with every make of machine.

Vanillen-Eis. — II.
(Vanilla Ice. — II.)

1 pint milk.	8 oz. sugar.
8 yolks.	Half a vanilla stick.

Mix ingredients and prepare the ice according to preceding recipe.

Sohokoladen-Eis
(Chocolate Ice.)

1 pint milk.	4 oz. sugar.
8 yolks.	3 oz. grated vanilla chocolate.
Prepare as Vanilla Ice.	

Nuss-Eis
(Nut Ice.)

1 pint milk.	8 oz. sugar.
8 yolks.	4 oz. grated candied hazelnuts.

Prepare as Vanilla Ice.

Kaffee-Eis
(Coffee Ice.)

2 oz. ground coffee.
1 pint milk.

8 yolks.
9 oz. sugar.

Boil up 2 oz. coarsely-ground coffee in the boiling milk and strain through a cloth. Then prepare as Vanilla Ice.

Zitronen-Eis
(Lemon Ice.)

1 pint water.
9 oz. sugar.

2 whites of eggs.
½ gill lemon juice.

The thinly-peeled rind of half a lemon.

Boil up the water with the lemon peel and sugar, then remove from the fire and take out the peel. Add the lemon juice and, when cold, stir in 2 whisked whites of eggs and freeze.

Erdbeer-Eis
(Strawberry Ice.)

1½ lb. wood strawberries.
½ pint water.
1 gill Rhine wine.

½ lb. sugar.
2 tablespoonsful lemon juice.
2 whites of eggs.

Rub the strawberries through a hair sieve. Boil up the water with the sugar and, when cold, stir into it the strawberries, lemon juice, wine and whisked whites of eggs and freeze.

Himbeer-Els
(Raspberry Ice.)

Prepared as Strawberry Ice, a little cochineal being added.

Eis von Schlagsahne
(Whipped Cream Ice.)

1 pint stiffly-whipped cream.
½ lb. sugar.

Half a vanilla stick, pounded.

Stir the cream, vanilla and sugar well together and fill the freezing machine at once with the mixture. All ice prepared with whipped cream need only stand 3 hours in a bed of ice — it need not be shaken.

Coffee extract or Maraschino may be substituted for the vanilla flavouring.

Gebäck: Torten und Kuchen
(Cakes.)

Napfkuchen mit Hefe
(Plain Yeast Cake.)

1¼ lb. sifted flour.	5 oz. sugar.	4 oz. raisins.
1½ oz. yeast.	5 oz. butter.	Lemon peel to taste.
½ pint milk.	4 oz. currants.	
3 eggs.	12 bitter almonds.	

Crumble up the yeast in a basin, sprinkle ½ teaspoonful of sugar over it and allow it to stand for 10 minutes. Then pour a gill of lukewarm milk on it, mix well and stir in sufficient of the sifted flour to make a paste. Stand in a warm place — not on the stove — to rise.

Beat the eggs and sugar to a froth, add the grated almonds and lemon peel and the butter (melted), then the risen prepared yeast and the remainder of the milk. Mix well, gradually add the flour, and then stir in the currants and raisins.

Beat this dough well with the rolling-pin till it no longer sticks to it. Well butter a fireproof earthenware mould (Napfkuchenform) or special cake tin made with a projection running up the middle allowing the heat to penetrate better. Line it with breadcrumbs and fill it half full with the dough. Stand in a warm place, covered over with a cloth, till it has risen to the top of the mould. Then put into the oven and bake 1 hour.

Abgeriebener Napfkuchen

1¼ lb. flour.	4 extra yolks.	3 oz. yeast.
½ lb. sugar.	10 oz. butter.	The rind of 1 lemon.
4 eggs.	4 oz. sultanas.	

Prepare the yeast as in preceding recipe, with a gill of the milk and 3 table-spoonsful flour. Cream the butter, beat it up with the eggs and sugar, add the sultanas and grated lemon peel and stir in the risen yeast. Add the milk and flour alternately, and knead the dough well. Fill, half full, a well-buttered earthenware mould (Napfkuchenform) lined with breadcrumbs, stand in a warm place, covered over, till the dough has well risen, and bake 1 hour.

¼ lb. grated sweet almonds may be substituted for the sultanas and lemon peel.

Striezel

2 lbs. flour.	2 oz. yeast.	5 oz. sugar.
4 eggs.	¾ pint milk.	7 oz. butter.

12 grated bitter almonds. ½ lb. currants.	½ lb. sultanas. 2 oz. candied peel.	A little grated lemon peel.

Prepare the yeast with the milk, 1 tablespoonful sugar and 4 tablespoonsful flour as in recipe "Napfkuchen" and allow to rise. Stir the beaten-up eggs into the flour and mix well with the butter (melted), the milk, sugar, almonds, candied and lemon peel and the risen yeast. Knead well and then add the currants and raisins. Form into small, long loaves, place on a buttered sheet of tin, leave to rise further, and then brush over with egg and bake ¾ to 1 hour. On taking out, brush over again with hot butter and sprinkle thickly with sugar.

Mohn-Striezel

For the dough:	In addition:
1½ lb. flour.	1 lb. blue poppy seeds.
2 oz. sugar.	2 oz. sweet almonds.
1 pint milk.	3 oz. butter.
2 oz. yeast.	6 oz. sugar.
3 oz. butter.	2 oz. currants.
2 eggs.	3 tablespoonsful milk.

Prepare the yeast as in "Napfkuchen" recipe with 1 lb. flour, the milk, flour, a little sugar and allow to rise. Then mix it well with the remaining flour, sugar and the butter (melted) and stand the dough to rise.

When well risen, roll out thinly, brush over with butter and spread on it a paste, made of the poppy seeds and other ingredients stated. Roll together and place on a sheet of tin, well-buttered and sprinkled with flour, to rise still further. Then brush over with egg and bake in a medium oven. When taken out of the oven, brush over again with hot butter and sprinkle thickly with sugar.

The poppy must be soaked for an hour, then boiled for 10 minutes in 1 pint milk, shaken on to a sieve to drain and pounded in a mortar before mixing with the other ingredients.

Butter-Zopf
(Butter Twist.)

1½ lb. flour. 3 oz. sugar. 2 oz. yeast.	½ pint milk. 2 eggs. 4 oz. butter.	8 bitter almonds. Grated rind of a lemon. Salt.

Prepare the yeast with the milk as in recipe "Napfkuchen" and allow to rise. Sift the flour, melt the butter and mix both with the beaten-up eggs, the sugar, risen yeast, grated almonds, lemon peel and a little salt. Knead well. Cut into long strips and loosely plait to a twist, broader in the middle than at the ends, which should be pinched together to a point. Allow to rise a little more and then brush over with butter and bake in a medium oven. On taking out of the oven, brush over again with butter and sprinkle thickly with sugar.

Stolle

2½ lbs. flour.	2 oz. candied peel.	¼ lb. currants.
1 pint milk.	2½ oz. yeast.	A little grated lemon
1 teaspoonful salt.	½ lb. butter.	peel.
¼ lb. raisins.	7 oz. sugar.	

Prepare the yeast as in recipe "Napfkuchen" with a gill of milk and ½ lb. flour and allow to rise. Stir the sugar and salt into the rest of the flour. Make a hole in the centre of it and pour in the milk, the butter (melted) and the risen yeast. Mix thoroughly and knead well. Add the currants, stoned raisins, and chopped candied peel and place in a pan to rise, covered over. When well risen, roll out to a long strip 2 to 3 inches thick, on a sheet of tin that has been well buttered and then sprinkled with flour. Brush over with butter and fold the two edges together to the middle. Allow to rise still further, then bake 1 hour in a hot oven. When taken out, brush at once with butter and sprinkle thickly with castor sugar.

4 oz. grated sweet almonds may be substituted for the raisins.

Kaffeekuchen

2 lbs. flour.	¾ lb. currants.	3 eggs.
1 pint milk.	14 oz. sugar.	Grated rind of 1 lemon.
1 lb. butter.	3 oz. yeast.	10 bitter almonds.

Prepare the yeast with ½ pint milk and a little of the flour, as in recipe "Napfkuchen." Allow to rise for 10 minutes. Mix with the remaining flour, 4 oz. sugar, the grated almonds and lemon peel, 10 oz. butter, the beaten-up eggs, milk, and lastly the risen yeast. Knead the dough well, then roll out, about ½ inch high, place on a buttered tin, and stand on one side to rise further. When about twice as high, brush over with the remaining 6 oz. butter (melted) and sprinkle over with the rest of the sugar. Bake 30 minutes in a hot oven and then cut up into pieces the desired size.

Mandelkuchen
(Almond Cake.)

¾ lb. butter.	6 eggs.	½ oz. baking powder.
3 oz. sweet almonds.	1 lb. flour.	
6 oz. sugar.	Grated rind of 1 lemon.	

Cream half the butter, then stir it well with the beaten-up yolks, sugar, grated lemon peel and the flour, the latter mixed with the baking powder and sifted.

Finally stir in the whisked whites of eggs. Spread about ¼ inch high on a buttered tin, sprinkle over with sugar and coarsely-chopped almonds, scatter the remaining butter in small lumps over it and bake in a moderate oven for 30 minutes.

Blechkuchen

1 lb. flour.	4 oz. butter.	½ pint milk.
2 eggs.	3 oz. sugar.	1½ oz. yeast.

Crumble the yeast into the lukewarm milk, mix well, pour into the centre of the flour in a basin, add the beaten-up eggs, the butter (melted) and sugar, and mix and knead well, beating with the rolling-pin till the paste no longer sticks to the latter. Stand in a covered pan in a warm place to rise. When well risen, cover with it — about 1 inch thick, or less — a well-buttered sheet of tin and let it rise a little longer before covering with fruit, etc., to make Obst-, Butter-, Streussel- or Käsekuchen.

Streusselkuchen

8 oz. flour.	1 teaspoonful cinnamon.
6 oz. butter (melted).	2 oz. grated almonds *or* vanilla (if
4 oz. sugar.	desired).

Prepare the dough as in preceding recipe "Blechkuchen," brush it over with a beaten-up egg and tablespoonful of creamed butter, and sprinkle thickly and equally with the following mixture, then baking as quickly as possible.

Mix the flour and sugar well. Melt the butter and add, mixing so that little lumps are formed; this is best done by rubbing between the palms of the hands.

Butterkachen

Prepare the dough as in recipe "Blechkuchen."

Let it rise well after being spread on the tin, press the surface in a little and put ½ lb. butter in little lumps all over it. Strew with ½ lb. castor sugar and bake a good brown in a quick oven.

Pflaumenkuchen

Prepare the dough as in recipe "Blechkuchen." Let it rise to about ½ inch or more on the sheet of tin, then brush over with 3 oz. butter (melted) and sprinkle with the same quantity of grated roll or dry breadcrumbs. Take 5 lbs. of plums, stone them, cut into quarters lengthwise and place them closely side by side on the dough. Bake ½ to ¾ hour, and sprinkle thickly with sugar immediately on taking out of the oven.

Kirschkuchen
(Cherry Cake.)

Prepare as Pflaumenkuchen, allowing 2 lbs. of stoned cherries, which should first have some of their juice pressed out of them.

Kasekuchen
(Cheese Cake.)

4 lbs. white milk cheese.	2 eggs.
3 oz. butter.	4 oz. currants.
4 oz. sugar.	A few bitter almonds.

Prepare the dough according to recipe "Blechkuchen," and arrange on a buttered tin with shallow turned-up edge. Allow to rise to twice its height, then mix all the above ingredients well and spread over the risen dough. Bake in a quick oven.

Apfelkuchen. — I.
(Apple Cake.)

Prepare as Pflaumenkuchen, allowing 3 lbs. apples, cut into slices.

Apfelkuchen. — II.
(Apple Cake.)

½ lb. flour.	Cinnamon.	1 egg.
½ oz. yeast.	3 oz. butter.	Apples or other fruit.
½ teaspoonful castor sugar.	½ gill lukewarm milk.	
	A little cream.	

Put ½ pound of flour in a basin, make a hole in the middle and pour in 3 ounces butter (melted), a little cream, ½ ounce yeast, and gteaspoonful castor sugar; mix with the yeast ½ gill lukewarm milk and 1 beaten-up egg.

Strain this into the middle of the flour, mix and knead all well together, cover the basin over and put it away to rise till it is twice its original size.

Then take the dough, roll it out thinly, and lay it on buttered tins or plates, spreading all over it melted butter, a good sprinkling of castor sugar and powdered cinnamon; cover thickly with apples peeled, cored, and cut into thick slices. Bake in a quick oven.

Other kinds of fruit may be used thus.

Apfelkuchen mit Blätterteig
(Apple Cake with Puff Paste.)

Make some puff paste with ½ lb. butter and ½ lb. flour.

Roll out thinly in two layers. Place one upon a buttered sheet of tin. Peel ¾ lb. apples, cut them into slices, stew them in ½ lb. sugar and ¼ pint water. Drain superfluous water off. Sprinkle over the paste on the tin with breadcrumbs, place the apples on it, cover with the other layer of paste, brush over with egg, sprinkle with sugar and bake in a moderate oven for ½ hour. Cut into squares and eat with whipped cream.

Blätterteig-Bretzel
(Puff Paste Twists.)

Make some puff paste, leave it in a cool place for some time, then roll it out and cut into strips about ½ inch thick and wide. Roll each strip on the well-floured board and twist into the shape of a Bretzel or double loop.

Bake a pale golden colour on a buttered tin.

Waffeln
(Wafers; *French:* Gaufres.)

¾ lb. flour.	4 oz. butter.	½ oz. baking powder.
2 oz. sugar.	½ pint milk.	4 grated bitter al-
3 eggs.	Grated rind of a lemon.	monds

Cream the butter, mix it with the sugar, beaten-up eggs, grated lemon rind and bitter almonds and, lastly, stir in alternately the milk and the flour, which should have been previously sifted and mixed with the baking powder. Heat a Waffeleisen (wafer iron) over a clear fire, rub it with a piece of bacon rind, pour a teaspoonful of the batter into each division and close up the iron again. Let the wafers become a golden colour, turning the iron so that both sides are done. Then take out and sprinkle over at once thickly with sugar.

Berliner Waffeln
(Berlin Wafers.)

8 oz. flour.	½ pint sour cream.
3 eggs.	2 tablespoonsful Kutnmel liqueur.
A little salt.	

Mix all ingredients and proceed as in preceding recipe.

Zimmet-Waffeln
(Cinnamon Wafers.)

½ lb. butter.	1 tablespoonful Maraschino.
4 eggs.	1 lb. sifted flour.
1 oz. cinnamon.	

Cream ½ lb. butter, beat up 4 eggs and stir into the butter, beating well. Flavour with 1 oz. cinnamon and 1 tablespoonful Maraschino. Then stir in 1 lb. sifted flour. Mix well. Grease and heat the special Waffeleisen (wafer irons), and proceed as in recipe "Waffeln."

Hefen-Waffeln
(Yeast Wafers.)

¾ lb. flour.	2 eggs.	A little grated lemon
1 oz. yeast.	1 pint milk.	peel.
6 oz. butter.		

Crumble the yeast, pour half of the milk, lukewarm, over it and stir in ¼ lb. of the flour. Stand on one side for at least 10 minutes to rise. Mix the remaining flour, milk, beaten-up eggs, butter and sugar and a little grated lemon peel and then add the risen yeast. Knead well and stand in a warm place to rise. When well risen, fill the greased and heated Waffeleisen with spoonsful and proceed as in previous recipes.

Konigskuchen
(King Cake.)

1 lb. butter.	½ oz. baking powder.	2 oz. sweet almonds.
1 lb. sugar.	Grated rind of a lemon.	8 bitter almonds.
¾ lb. flour.	8 eggs.	2 oz. candied peel.
¼ lb. potato flour.	½ lb. currants.	1 tablespoonful rum.

Cream the butter, then add the sugar and yolks and stir all ¾ hour. Next add the grated lemon peel, almonds, chopped candied peel and rum and stir in alternately the sifted flour, mixed with baking powder and the whisked whites of eggs. Stir in lightly, last of all, the currants well washed and dried, fill a long, square tin (tin-loaf shape) and bake 1 to 1¼ hour.

Tausendjahrkuchen
(Thousand Year Cake.)

1 lb. currants.	1 lb. butter.
1 lb. flour.	1 lb. sugar.
8 eggs.	Grated rind of 1 lemon

Cream the butter, stir three-fourths of the flour into it and beat for 1 hour to a froth. In another basin beat, also to a froth, the sugar and yolks. Add the grated lemon peel and then the whites, whisked stiffly. Then mix with the beaten-up flour and butter and finally stir in lightly the well-washed and dried currants. Fill a well-buttered cake tin and bake 1 to 1¼ hour.

Süste

¼ lb. butter.	4 bitter almonds.	1 oz. baking powder.
¼ lb. sugar.	2 oz. sweet almonds.	
4 eggs.	¾ lb. flour.	

Cream the butter. Stir in the sugar and grated almonds and then alternately a beaten-up egg and a heaped tablespoonful of flour, mixing well. The flour should be mixed with the baking powder and then sifted. Fill a well-buttered cake tin and bake 1 hour.

Altdeutscher Napfkuchen

1 lb. clarified butter,	8 eggs.
1¼ lb. sifted flour.	¾ lb. sugar.
½ oz. baking powder.	¾ lb. currants.
A little cardamom.	Grated rind of a lemon.

Cream the butter and the sugar and then add the yolks of eggs. Beat ¾ hour to a froth, then add the grated lemon peel and cardamom and alternately the whites of eggs, whisked to a snow, and the sifted flour, mixed with the baking powder. Finally stir in the currants lightly. Bake about 1¼ hour.

Berliner Pfannkachen
(Berlin Pancakes.)

1 lb. flour.	8 bitter almonds.
2 oz. sugar.	1 tablespoonful rum,
4 eggs.	½ pint milk.
4 oz. butter.	1½ oz. yeast.

Crumble the yeast, sprinkle a little sugar over it and stir it with ½ gill milk and 3 tablespoonsful flour. Stand on one side for 10 minutes to rise.

Beat the sugar and eggs to a froth, stir into them by degrees the grated almonds, rum, flour, butter (melted), prepared yeast, and remaining milk, mixing thoroughly. Knead and beat the dough and place in a covered pan near the fire to rise. Then take a piece of the dough, place it on a floured pasteboard and draw out a strip to about ½ inch in thickness. On this, at intervals of about 2 inches from one another and from the edge, place with a teaspoon, small heaps of jam, mixed with a little rum. Fold the edges of the strip of dough together, so that the jam is completely covered, and press together a little round each heap of the jam. Then with a wine glass cut out the doughnuts, leaving a good margin round the jam. Press the edges together firmly and place on another floured board to rise. Continue in this manner until the whole of the dough has been made into doughnuts. When they have well risen, slide them carefully, three or four at a time, into a large saucepan of steaming hot fat and leave them in till brown on all sides. To test if done, insert a wooden skewer; if dry when withdrawn, the doughnuts are ready to take out. Place them then on a sieve, on blotting paper, to absorb all fat and afterwards on a dish, rolling them first in fine castor sugar.

Instead of the sugar, a thin icing may be poured over them, composed of 1 lb. castor sugar mixed with a gill of rosewater.

Spritzkuchen

2 oz. butter.	1½ oz. sugar.
¾ pint water.	6 eggs.
A pinch of salt.	Some grated lemon peel *or* grated
½ lb. sifted flour.	almonds.

Put the water into a saucepan with the butter, and, as soon as it boils, stir in the sugar, lemon peel, salt and flour, and heat, stirring well, till all becomes a firm, dry mass. Remove from the fire and stir in at once 2 beatenup eggs. When nearly cool, add gradually the remaining 4 eggs. Fill a special cake syringe (Kuchenspritze) three-quarters full with this paste.

Bring 2 lbs. of frying fat to the boil. Take small pieces of paper (about 4 inches square), dip them into the boiling fat, and then press out from the syringe a ring of paste on to each paper, joining the ends of the ring together, so that they do not open out again. Slide the papers into the fat, a few at a time. As the paste rings touch the fat, they come away from the paper and swell out. When they begin to show cracks on the upper side and appear a light brown, turn them and let the other side finish browning. On taking out, dip into a mixture of castor sugar and rosewater, so that they receive a glaze on their upper sides. To make this icing, mix 1 gill rosewater with 1 lb. castor sugar.

Kaffeekringel

2 oz. butter.	¾ lb. flour.	½ teaspoonful baking
3 oz. sugar.	2 eggs.	powder.

Beat the eggs well with the butter and sugar, then stir in the flour, sifted and mixed with the baking powder, and mix thoroughly to a firm dough. Form into rings and other shapes and throw into steaming hot fat. When a light brown, take out and drain on blotting paper over a sieve.

Polniscber Krengel

4 eggs.	1 teaspoonful salt.	1 gill creamed butter.
½ pint milk.	1½ lb. flour.	1 oz. yeast.

In addition:

¾ lb. butter.	Grated rind of 1 lemon.
¼ lb. sugar.	1 lb. currants *or* 1 lb. grated almonds.

Dissolve the yeast in the lukewarm milk, sift the flour and stir it in with the creamed butter and beaten-up eggs. Mix very thoroughly. Make a serviette very wet in cold water, wring it out and well butter the centre of it. Place the dough on this and then tie firmly together, allowing plenty of room for the dough to rise. Then put into a pail of cold water overnight. Next day remove the cloth and roll out very thinly. Sprinkle over with currants or ½ lb. sultanas, or ¼ lb. grated almonds, with ¾ lb. butter, in little lumps, ¼ lb. sugar and the grated rind of a lemon. Roll together and form into a twisted Bretzel, or looped twist. Stand to rise for 2 vhours in a warm pan, then brush over with egg, sprinkle with sugar, and bake in a moderate oven for 30 minutes.

Plunderbretzel. — Kranzkuchen

1½ lb. flour.	½ lb. sultanas.	4 oz. sweet almonds.
¾ lb. butter.	1 egg.	Grated rind of ½ lem-
2 oz. yeast.	3 extra yolks.	on.
½ pint milk.	8 oz. sugar.	

Mix the flour, lukewarm milk, yeast, 1 egg and the 3 extra yolks, ¼ lb. butter and ¼ lb. sugar well and stand, covered over, in a warm place to rise. Then place the dough on a floured pasteboard and roll out about ½ inch thick. Press the rest of the butter to a firm square lump, place in the middle of the rolled-out paste and fold the latter over it. Roll out well, then turn the corners to the centre again, press together and roll out once more. Repeat this process several times and then stand in a cool place for ½ hour. Then roll out again to about ¼ inch thick and 18 inches long, and sprinkle over with the remaining ¼ lb. sugar, grated lemon peel and the sultanas and chopped almonds. Roll together, form into a looped twist (Bretzel) or circle (Kranz), and place on a buttered sheet of tin. When risen, bake in a brisk oven. On taking out, brush over with butter and sprinkle with sugar and cinnamon.

Blitzkuchen
(Lightning Cake.)

½ lb. sugar.	½ lb. potato	½ oz. baking	6 eggs.
½ lb. butter.	flour mixed with	powder.	½ lb. flour.

Grated rind and | juice of a lemon.

Cream the butter and stir into it the beaten-up eggs, sugar, lemon juice and grated lemon peel, and lastly add the flour, sifted, and mixed with baking powder. When thoroughly mixed, fill at once a well-buttered tin and bake 1 hour.

Butter-Mandel-Torte
(Almond Spongecake.)

1 lb. butter.	1 lb. sugar.	1 lb. flour.
½ lb. sweet almonds.	½ oz. baking powder.	½ gill rum.
8 bitter almonds.	Grated rind of 1 lemon.	8 eggs.

Cream the butter, add the beaten-up eggs and sugar and stir for ¾ hour. Then add the grated lemon peel and almonds, the rum, half of the flour, mixed with baking powder, and half of the whites of eggs, whisked stiffly. When well mixed, add the remaining flour and whisked whites. Fill a well-buttered tin and bake 1 to 1¼ hour. The substitution of hazelnuts for almonds is a great improvement.

Biscuit-Torte
(Spongecake.)

1 teaspoonful grated lemon peel.	4 oz. cornflour *or* potato flour,
8 oz. sugar.	1 tablespoonful lemon juice.
8 eggs.	

Stir the beaten-up eggs with the sugar, lemon juice and grated lemon peel, in a double milk saucepan, to a froth. Then sprinkle in the cornflour or potato flour, stirring briskly all the time. Fill at once a wide, shallow tin, well-buttered and bake 1 hour in a moderate oven. Ten minutes after taking out of the oven, turn out and glaze with icing. The cake may be cut through when cold into two layers, jam spread on the under half and the top then placed on it again.

Schokoladen-Biscuit
(Chocolate Spongecake.)

5 oz. cornflour.	3 oz. grated chocolate.
6 oz. sugar.	6 eggs.

Whisk the whites of eggs stiffly, then stir into them the beaten-up yolks, sugar, grated chocolate and cornflour. Fill a well-buttered cake tin and bake 1 hour.

Sacher-Torte

| ½ lb. chocolate. | ½ lb. butter. | 2 oz. potato flour. |
| ½ lb. castor sugar. | ½ lb. sweet almonds. | 8 eggs. |

Cream the butter, add the beaten-up yolks and sugar, and stir for ¾ hour. Then stir in alternately the flour (mixed with the grated almonds) and the whites, whisked stiffly. Fill a well-buttered tin and bake about an hour. Cover with chocolate icing.

Triester Torte

½ lb. butter.	½ lb. almonds, grated	2 oz. grated roll *or* dry
6 eggs.	with the skins.	breadcrumbs.
¼ lb. chocolate.	½ lb. sugar.	

Cream the butter, add the beaten-up yolks and sugar gradually, the grated almonds and chocolate, and finally the grated roll and the whites of eggs, whisked stiffly. Fill a well-buttered tin and bake in a slow oven.

Linzer Torte

1 lb. flour.	2 tablespoonsful rum.	10 bitter almonds.
10 oz. butter.	10 oz. sugar.	
½ lb. blanched, grated	5 eggs.	
sweet almonds.	Jam.	

Cream the butter, then add the beaten-up eggs, sugar, almonds, rum and flour. Stir well, working the paste with the hands finally. Leave in a cool place for an hour, then roll out, place on two buttered sheets of tin and bake a light brown. Allow to cool, spread jam on one portion, cover with the other, and spread over the top layer any icing desired.

Wiener Torte

| 1 lb. flour, | ¾ lb. butter. | 4 whites of eggs. |
| ¾ lb. sugar. | 6 yolks. | Grated rind of a lemon. |

Cream the butter, add sugar and the beaten-up yolks, and stir ¾ hour. Then add the grated lemon peel and alternately the flour, and whisked whites of eggs. Roll out in three pieces and bake on buttered tins. Place the layers on each other, spreading jam between.

Lagen-Torte

| 1 lb. flour. | ¼ lb. sugar. | 4 boiled yolks. |
| ¾ lb. firm butter. | 6 raw yolks. | |

Sift the flour, pull the butter into small pieces, add to the flour, stir in the sugar and the rubbed hard-boiled yolks, the 6 well-beaten raw yolks, and mix thoroughly and quickly to a paste. Roll out into four pieces, bake on buttered sheets of tin, spread three of them each with a different jam and spread an icing of any kind over the top.

Gries-Torte
(Ground Rice Spongecake.)

10 oz. ground rice.	1 lb. sugar.
10 bitter almonds.	Grated peel and the juice of ½ lem-
4 oz. sweet almonds.	on.
10 eggs.	

Beat the yolks and sugar to a froth and add the grated almonds and sugar. Stir all for 1 hour and then add alternately the ground rice and the whites of eggs, whisked stiffly. Fill a well-buttered cake tin and bake 1 hour. The cake may be cut through when cold and a layer of jam spread on the under half, the top then being placed on it again.

Pumpernickel-Torte
(Pumpernickel Spongecake.)

4 oz. grated Pumper-	10 bitter almonds.	1 lb. sugar.
nickel.	10 eggs.	2 ground cloves.
4 oz. sweet almonds,	Grated rind of 1 lemon,	

Beat the sugar with the eggs for ½ hour to a thick cream. Then add the grated almonds and spice, and finally the grated Pumpernickel which must be very dry. Glaze with sugar or chocolate icing.

Baum-Torte
(Tree Spongecake.)

1 lb. sugar.	14 oz. flour.
10 eggs	4 oz. potato flour *or* cornflour.
2 to 3 grains cardamom.	4 oz. sweet almonds,
A little vanilla.	10 bitter almonds.
The grated rind of a lemon.	1 tablespoonful rum.
A small piece of mace.	

Cream the butter, add the sugar and beaten-up yolks of eggs and stir all for ¾ hour. Then add the grated lemon peel, the almonds (grated in their skin), and the ground spice, adding then, alternately, the flour, sifted and mixed with baking powder and the whites of eggs whisked stiffly. Mix well. Butter a broad, shallow cake tin (Tortenform), line it with buttered paper, and pour sufficient of the mixture in to thinly cover the bottom. Place in the oven for a few minutes till slightly brown, then pour in enough to make another layer and bake as before, placing the tin now, however, on a pan of cold water, which must be renewed with fresh cold water immediately it begins to boil. This is to prevent the cake becoming overdone at the bottom. A few sheets of tin may also be placed under the cake tin. As each layer is baked, add another, until all of the mixture has been used up.

Chocolate, or any other, icing may be spread over the cake, which may also be ornamented with marzipan, etc. A richer cake is obtained by baking three-quarters of the mixture on layers as described and then taking out of the tin. The rest of the mixture is then baked in two layers. Spread on the thicker portion a layer of good jam, cover with a layer of marzipan, and place the thinner layer of cake on this. Glaze with lemon icing and ornament with marzipan fruit or preserved fruit. For the layer of marzipan reckon ½ lb. sweet almonds, ½ lb. castor sugar and ½ gill rose water. (*See* recipe.)

Schokoladen-Torte
(Chocolate Cake.)

2 oz. almonds, grated in their skins.	4 oz. chocolate dissolved in 2 table-
4 tablespoonsful flour.	spoonsful water.
4 oz. butter.	Vanilla flavouring.
4 eggs.	

Cream the butter, add the sugar and beaten-up yolks and stir for ½ hour. Then add the flour, chocolate, grated almonds and the vanilla flavouring. Mix well and finally stir in the well-whisked whites of eggs. Fill a well-buttered cake tin and bake in a moderate oven for 1 hour.

Rehrücken
(Saddle of Venison. — A Viennese Cake.)

6 oz. butter.	2 oz. almonds, grated in their skins.
6 eggs.	2 oz. flour.
4 oz. sugar.	4 oz. chocolate.

Cream the butter, add the sugar and yolks of eggs and stir for ¾ hour. Then add the grated almonds and alternately the flour and whisked whites of eggs. Fill a special, long cake tin (obtainable from Lademann and Sohne, Wallstrasse, Berlin) and bake 1 hour. As soon as cool, cover with chocolate icing and ornament with blanched almonds, cut into strips.

Sand-Torte
(Spongecake.)

1 lb. clarified butter,	1 lb. sugar.	The grated rind of 1
¾ lb. potato flour.	½ gill rum.	lemon.
¼ lb. wheaten flour,	8 bitter almonds or	
10 eggs.	vanilla flavouring.	

Cream the butter, add to it 2 eggs beaten-up whole and 8 yolks and stir continuously for ¾ hour. Then add the grated lemon rind and bitter almonds, and the rum. Stir in half of the two kinds of flour, mixed, and half of the whites of eggs, whisked stiffly. When thoroughly mixed, add the remainder of the whisked whites and flour. Fill a well-buttered cake tin and bake 1 to 1¼ hour. A little baking powder may be added to the flour.

Mohn-Torte
(Poppy Cake.)

½ lb. white poppy	¾ pint milk.	¾ lb. sugar.
seeds.	¼ lb. sweet almonds.	8 eggs.

Scald the poppy seeds, boil in the milk and drain on a sieve. Then pound in a mortar. Beat the sugar and yolks to a froth, add the poppy seeds and grated almonds and, lastly, stir in the stiffly-whisked whites of eggs. Fill a well-buttered shallow tin (with movable bottom) lined with breadcrumbs and bake in a moderate oven for 1 hour.

Nuss-Torte
(Nut Cake.)

¾ lb. nuts.	¾ lb. sugar.
10 eggs.	A few bitter almonds.

Beat the sugar and yolks to a froth, then stir in alternately the grated nuts and whisked whites of eggs. Bake 1 hour in well-buttered tin. Spread with sugar or chocolate icing, and ornament with candied walnuts or hazelnuts.

½ lb. hazelnuts and ¼ lb. sweet almonds may be taken instead of the whole quantity of hazelnuts.

Apfel-Torte

6 oz. butter.	6 oz. sugar.	2 tablespoonsful sour
1 egg.	4 oz. currants.	cream.
2 yolks.	10 oz. flour.	2 oz. sweet almonds.
2 lbs. apples.		

In addition: ½ gill sour cream, a little extra sugar, and 4 yolks.

Cream the butter, add 1 egg, 2 extra yolks, 2 oz. sugar, 1 tablespoonful water and then the flour and mix to a paste. Roll out and line the bottom and sides of a shallow, broad, cake tin. Bake a few minutes, but not completely. Grate the almonds and mix with 2 tablespoonsful of sour cream. Spread on the cake and sprinkle over with grated breadcrumbs.

Peel the apples, cut them into thin slices and mix with the currants and 4 oz. sugar. Place these on the breadcrumbs and pour over them ½ gill of slightly sour cream, beaten up with 4 yolks and a little sugar. Place in the oven and finish baking.

Stachelbeer-Torte
(Gooseberry Cake.)

Prepare the paste as for Apfel-Torte. When baked, spread almond paste over it and dry grated breadcrumbs. Then put on it 2 lbs. gooseberries, which have just been brought to the boil, but remain whole, drained well and rolled in sugar. Cover the fruit with the whites of eggs, stiffly whisked with 2 oz. castor sugar, and bake a further 5 minutes.

Kirsch-Torte
(Cherry Cake.)

½ lb. flour.	½ oz. baking powder.
¼ lb. potato flour.	½ lb. sugar.
½ lb. butter.	5 tablespoonsful dry breadcrumbs.
1½ lb. cherries, stoned and some of	6 eggs.
the juice pressed out.	Grated rind of a lemon.

Cream the butter, then add the sugar, beaten-up eggs, grated lemon peel and finally the flour mixed with the baking powder. Stir well together. Fill a well-buttered cake tin with half this quantity, strew in 3 tablespoonsful dry breadcrumbs, lay the cherries on this, sprinkle another 2 tablespoonsful breadcrumbs over them, and then cover with the remainder of the paste. Bake about 1 hour.

Stoned, skinned plums may be substituted for the cherries.

Mandel-Torte
(Almond Cake.)

1 lb. sugar.	1 lb. sweet almonds.
10 bitter almonds.	4 oz. potato flour.
8 eggs.	

Blanch the almonds and grate them finely. Beat the sugar and yolks ½ to ¾ hour to a froth and stir in alternately the potato flour, whisked whites of eggs and grated almonds.

Fill a well-buttered tin and bake 1 hour.

Teegeback
(Tea Biscuits.)

Loffelbiskuit

3 eggs. The weight of 3 eggs in flour and in sugar.

Beat the yolks with the sugar to a froth and stir in alternately the flour and the whites of eggs, whisked stiffly. Place a piece of well-buttered white paper on a sheet of tin. Twist a sheet of white paper into the shape of a funnel, cut off the tip, fill with the batter and sprinkle on to the buttered paper in little strips about 4 inches long. Dust over with castor sugar and bake a golden colour.

Dessertbiskait

The weight of 4 eggs in sugar.	2 yolks of eggs.
The weight of 2 eggs in flour.	4 whites of eggs.

Whisk the whites of eggs stiffly, then stir in lightly the beaten-up yolks, and with a wooden spoon mix with the sugar, and lastly the flour. As in last recipe, sprinkle the paste through the end of a paper funnel into the shape of rings or fingers on to a buttered sheet of paper laid on a sheet of tin. Dust over with castor sugar and bake a pale golden colour.

Kleine Biskuittörtchen

3 eggs.	2 oz. grated sweet almonds.
7 oz. castor sugar.	4 oz. potato flour.

Beat the eggs and sugar to a froth and stir in the grated almonds and potato flour. Fill little patty pans, buttered and dusted over with potato flour and bake in a moderate oven.

Aniskuchen
(Aniseed Cakes.)

4 oz. sugar.	1 teaspoonful aniseed.
4 eggs.	4 oz. flour.

Beat the eggs and sugar ½ hour to a froth, then add the pounded aniseed, and gradually the sifted flour. Put into little heaps (with at least 6 inches between each) on a well-buttered sheet of tin and bake in a moderate oven, after standing 2 hours.

Zimmetplätzchen
(Cinnamon Cakes.)

6 oz. butter.	1 yolk.	½ lb. cornflour.
2 oz. flour.	6 oz. sugar.	
2 eggs.	½ oz. ground ginger.	

Cream the butter, then add the sugar and stir a further 10 minutes. Add the eggs and cinnamon and then mix well with the flour. Make up into little rolls, 1 inch thick and 3 to 4 inches long, and bake on a buttered tin, in a moderate oven.

Eierplätzchen

2 hard-boiled yolks.	10 oz. flour.	4 oz. sugar.
4 oz. butter.	2 raw yolks.	

Beat the raw yolks well and stir into them the rubbed hard-boiled yolks. Then add the butter, sugar and lastly the flour. Mix well, roll out and cut with a cutter into various shapes. Brush over with yolk of egg, sprinkle with sugar and cinnamon and bake on a well-buttered tin.

Kleine Sandkuchen

1 lb. butter.	½ lb. potato flour.	Lemon *or* vanilla flavouring.
1 lb. sugar.	8 eggs.	
1 lb. wheaten flour.		

Cream the butter, add the sugar and beaten-up eggs and stir all together ½ hour. Add the flavouring and lastly the flour, gradually. Put into little heaps on a buttered sheet of tin and bake at once in a hot oven to a golden colour.

Mandelspäne
(Almond Chips.)

1 lb. sweet almonds.	1 oz. potato flour.
1 lb. sugar.	2 whites of eggs.

Beat the whites and sugar for 10 minutes, then stir in the flour and grated almonds and mix well. Spread 1 inch thick on rice paper and bake on a buttered tin in a moderate oven. Remove at once from tin and, while warm, twist round a rolling pin to dry in a curve.

Mürbekuchen.— I.

½ lb. butter.	¾ lb. flour.
4 tablespoonsful sweet cream.	2 oz. sugar.

176

Cream the butter, and mix well with the cream, sugar and flour. Roll out, cut into various shapes with a cutter, brush over with egg, sprinkle with sugar and bake a pale yellow on a buttered tin.

Mürbekuchen.— II.

½ lb. butter.	3 eggs.	Vanilla *or* lemon fla-
½ lb. sugar.	½ oz. baking powder.	vouring.
1 lb. flour.		

Cream the butter, and then stir in the sugar, beaten-up eggs, flavouring and the flour, sifted and mixed with baking powder. Stand the paste on one side for a time, then roll out and proceed as in previous recipe.

Teekuchen
(Tea Biscuits.)

½ lb. butter.	2 eggs.
¼ lb. sugar.	Ground vanilla.
1 lb. flour.	Chopped almonds.
2 tablespoonsful water.	

Cream the butter, add the sugar, eggs, beaten-up, water and plenty of vanilla, and lastly the flour. Roll out very thin, cut into various shapes, brush over with white of eggs, or butter, sprinkle with sugar and chopped almonds and bake a pale brown on a buttered tin.

Kleine Kirschtörtchen
(Cherry Tartlets.)

½ lb. flour.	1 tablespoonful dry breadcrumbs.
2 lbs. stoned sour cherries.	2 tablespoonsful milk.
3 oz. butter.	1 egg.

Mix the butter, sugar and flour well, make a hollow in the middle and pour in the egg, beaten up with the milk. Mix thoroughly and let the paste stand 15 minutes in a cool place. Then roll out about 1/3 inch thick and cut into rounds. Place a little edging of the paste on each round to form a rim. Sprinkle with dry grated breadcrumbs, fill with cherries, dusted over with sugar, and bake in a hot oven. Sprinkle well with sugar before eating.

Gooseberry tartlets are prepared in the same manner, the gooseberries being first just brought to the boil and then drained.

Kümmel-Kakes
(Carraway Biscuits.)

1 lb. flour.	½ pint milk.
½ oz. baking powder.	½ lb. cornflour.
½ oz. ground carraway seed.	½ lb. butter.
1 oz. salt.	

Cream the butter and stir in the flour, salt and ground carraway. Then add the milk and mix thoroughly. Roll out ½ inch thick, cut into various shapes with a cutter, sprinkle over with salt and carraway and bake in a hot oven.

To be eaten buttered, with slices of cheese or cold meat laid on.

Kümmelstangen
(Carraway Sticks.)

½ lb. flour.	1 tablespoonful milk.
I teaspoonful Parmesan cheese.	1 extra yolk.
3 oz. butter.	A pinch of white pepper.
1 teaspoonful salt.	Ground carraway.
1 egg.	½ oz. baking powder.

Cream the butter, stir in the yolks, salt, pepper, milk, cheese, (which may also be omitted, if preferred), and lastly the flour, sifted with the baking powder. Form into little rolls, about 2 inches long and ½ inch thick, brush over with the beaten-up egg, sprinkle thickly with carraway and bake in a cool oven.

Makronen
(Macaroons.)

½ lb. sugar.	½ lb. sweet almonds, grated.
3 whites of eggs.	A few bitter almonds.

Beat the whites to a snow and mix well with the sugar. Then add the almonds, blanched and grated, and should the paste be too moist, add a few dry breadcrumbs. Place in little heaps on a buttered tin and bake a pale brown.

Nussmakronen
(Nut Macaroons.)

1 lb. sugar.	6 eggs.
1 lb. hazelnut kernels.	6 bitter almonds.

Beat the sugar and eggs to a froth, mix in the finely-grated nuts and almonds, put in little heaps on a well-buttered sheet of tin and bake in a brisk oven. The macaroons should be soft in the centre.

Weihnachts-Gebäck

(Christmas Cakes.)

Marzipan
(Marchpane.)

1 lb. sweet almonds.
1 lb. castor sugar.

1 oz. bitter almonds.
4 tablespoonsful rosewater.

Blanch the almonds and grate them finely. Then mix them well with the sugar and rosewater, kneading well, so that the paste can be easily rolled out. Form into a ball and leave for some hours, before working up into various shapes or spreading, thinly rolled out, on Torten or Pfefferkuchen.

Honigkuchen. — I.
(Honey Cakes. — I.)

1 lb. honey.
2 lbs. flour.
½ lb. sugar.
3 whole eggs.
2 oz. butter.
1 tablespoonful rum.

1 teaspoonful ground cinnamon.
1 teaspoonful potash.
A little ground ginger.
A little ground mace.
2 oz. chopped candied peel.
A little grated lemon peel.

Warm the honey sufficiently for the butter to melt in it. Dissolve the potash in the rum and add it also to the honey. Shake the flour into a basin, make a hollow in the middle, pour into it the beaten-up eggs, the lukewarm honey and the remaining ingredients. Mix well and knead to a firm paste. Roll out very thinly, cut into various shapes with a cutter, place on a buttered tin and bake a light brown. The cakes may also be brushed over with white of egg and sprinkled with chopped almonds.

Honigkuchen. — II.
(Honey Cake. — II.)

1 lb. honey.
½ lb. sugar.
½ gill rosewater.
½ oz. potash.
1½ lb. flour.
3 eggs.

½ lb. chopped hazelnut kernels.
5 ground cloves.
½ oz. cinnamon, ground.
½ tablespoonful grated lemon peel.
16 grated bitter almonds.

Mix the flour, chopped hazelnuts, cinnamon, cloves, lemon peel and almonds. Boil up the honey with the sugar and when cool, pour into the flour and spice, with the potash dissolved in ½ gill rosewater and beaten up with the 3 eggs. Mix well and knead with the hands. Immediately the paste begins to stiffen, roll it out about ½ inch thick and bake in a moderate oven on a buttered tin with a turned-up edge. Cut up and ornament with a thin sugar icing (*see* Spritzglasur). Before baking the cake, sliced almonds and strips of candied peel may be arranged on it.

Pfefferkuchen
(Gingerbread.)

5 eggs.	6 oz. mixed peel.
6 powdered cloves.	¼ lb. sweet almonds.
½ grated nutmeg.	¼ oz. carbonate of soda.
¼ oz. ground ginger.	¼ teaspoonful ground cinnamon.
9 oz. castor sugar.	2 tablespoonsful milk.

Whisk the eggs in a basin and add to them the cloves, nutmeg, cinnamon and castor sugar. Beat these well for about 10 minutes.

Next add the peel, cut into thin but rather large pieces, the flour well dried, the almonds, blanched and cut into halves, and carbonate of soda mixed in 2 tablespoonsful of milk.

Stir quickly and pour into a deep baking tin lined with butter, or, which is much better, wafer papers.

Shake some more almonds on the top and bake in a moderate oven, three-quarters of an hour. When nearly done, sprinkle a little icing sugar on the top.

This will keep well in a dry tin.

Dicker Pfefferkuchen mit Honig
(Ginger Cake with Honey.)

3 lbs. honey.	2 teaspoonsful rosewater.
½ lb. sugar.	3 lbs. flour.
Grated rind of 1 lemon.	½ lb. chopped almonds.
½ oz. ground cardamom.	¼ lb. butter.
½ oz. ground cloves.	½ oz. ground ginger.
1½ oz. potash.	½ oz. ground cinnamon.
Candied peel to taste.	

Boil up the sugar and honey and pour into a basin. When a little cool, mix in the flour, the remaining ingredients and the potash dissolved in 2 teaspoonsful rosewater. Work up into a firm dough and leave in a cool place for 3 weeks.

Roll out about an inch thick, place on sheets of buttered tin, brush over with white of egg, whisked with rosewater, and bake a nice brown. Cut up while warm.

Sohwäbische Pfefferkuchen
(Swabian Pepperbread.)

1 lb. flour.
½ lb. sugar.
5 eggs.
½ pint honey,
¼ lb. butter.
5 to 6 peppercorns.
The grated rind of a lemon.

4 grains of cardamom.
½ oz. potash dissolved in 2 tablespoonsful rosewater.
½ gill rum.
2 oz. candied peel.
A pinch of ground cinnamon.
10 ground cloves.

Beat the eggs and sugar to a froth, stir in all the spices, the chopped candied peel and rum and stir 15 minutes. Then add the honey, in which the butter has been warmed, the potash (dissolved in 2 tablespoonsful rosewater) and lastly the flour, stirred in gradually. Fill a well-buttered cake tin, lined with buttered paper, and bake for 1 hour. Ornament the top of the cake with slices of candied peel and of almonds.

Bomben

Add to the ingredients in the preceding recipe 1 lb. chopped almonds, an additional 2 oz. candied peel, 1 lb. currants and 2 oz. cocoa and fill little 1 lb. buttered tins. Bake in a medium oven for f hour and then ice with chocolate icing.

Weisse Pfefferkuchen

5 eggs.
½ teaspoonful potash dissolved in 2
tablespoonsful milk.
1 lb. flour.

12 oz. sugar.
3 oz. candied peel.
10 ground cloves.

Beat the sugar and eggs for 30 minutes to a froth. Then add the potash dissolved in milk, the finelychopped candied peel, ground cloves and the flour gradually and stir 30 minutes. Roll out thinly, cut into little shapes and place on a floured tin till the next day. Before baking, brush over with egg and ornament with slices of candied peel and of almonds. 4 oz. grated sweet almonds and 15 bitter almonds may be substituted for the chopped candied peel and ground cloves.

Weisse Pfeffernüsse

1 lb. sugar.
1 lb. flour.

4 eggs.
4 oz. almonds.

Candied peel *or* vanilla.

Beat the sugar and eggs to a froth for half an hour. Then add the flavouring and stir in the flour, kneading well. Make up into little rolls, ½ to 1 inch in thickness. Cut into slices slantingly, place on a buttered tin and bake in a moderate oven.

Weisse runde Pfeffernüsse

½ lb. butter.	2 lbs. flour.	1 teaspoonful baking
1 gill milk.	4 eggs.	powder.
1 lb. sugar.	Spices to taste.	

Cream the butter, add the sugar, beaten-up eggs and spices, the baking powder, dissolved in the milk and the sifted flour stirred in gradually. Mix and knead well. Make into little round nuts and bake on a buttered tin till quite dry throughout.

Braune Pfeffernüsse
(Mecklenbargische.)

1 lb. syrup.	½ oz. ground cinnamon.
½ lb. sugar,	10 oz. ground cloves.
1½ oz. butter.	1 tablespoonful chopped candied or-
½ oz. potash dissolved in 4 table-	ange peel.
spoonsful rosewater.	4 oz. chopped citron.
1 teaspoonful ground coriander.	A pinch of baking powder.
2 lbs. flour.	

Boil up the syrup, sugar and butter. Mix 1½ lb. flour (mixed with the baking powder) with the ground spices, and chopped candied peel. Add the cooled syrup and the potash, dissolved in rosewater. Then stir in the remaining flour and knead to a dough. Cover over and leave in a warm place for 3 days, kneading it again on the second day. Make up into rolls, slice them up slantingly and bake on a buttered tin in a moderate oven.

Gewürzplätzchen
(Spiced Drops.)

1½ lb. flour.	¼ oz. potash.	½ oz. ground dried
¼ lb. butter.	½ oz. ground ginger.	bitter orange peel.
¼ oz. ground cloves.	2 lbs. syrup.	½ oz. ground cinna-
¼ oz. cardamom.	½ lb. sugar.	mon.

Boil up the syrup with the sugar. When a little cool, stir in the butter, spice, and flour, and the potash dissolved in rosewater. Mix together and knead well. Leave some days to stand. Before baking, roll out very thinly, cut into various shapes and bake a light brown on a buttered tin.

Zuckerplätzohen
(Sugar Drops.)

½ lb. castor sugar.	3 eggs.	Sugar for sprinkling
½ lb. flour.	Vanilla.	over with.

Beat the eggs 30 minutes with the sugar, then add the flour gradually and stir a few minutes longer. Arrange in little rough heaps on a buttered tin, and bake in a moderate oven. Sprinkle over with sugar.

Springer

1 lb. castor sugar.	4 eggs.
The rind of a lemon.	1 lb. flour.

Beat the yolks well with the sugar and lemon peel, then stir in the whisked whites and the flour. Roll out thinly, cut into little shapes and stand in a cool place for 6 hours. Place on a buttered tin and bake in a moderate oven. The addition of 4 oz. sweet almonds and a few bitter almonds finely grated is an improvement.

Mandelschnitten
(Almond Biscuits.)

½ lb. butter.	1 egg.
¾ lb. flour.	2 oz. finely-chopped almonds,
The rind of a lemon	4 oz. sugar for sprinkling over with.
4 oz. grated almonds	A pinch of baking powder.

Mix all ingredients well together to a paste. Roll out ½ inch thick, brush over with white of egg., sprinkle thickly with the 2 oz. chopped almonds and the sugar, cut into diamond-shaped pieces and bake in a moderate oven.

Wiener Kipfel

5 oz. butter.	2 oz. sugar.	Vanilla flavouring.
6 oz. flour.	2 oz. sweet almonds.	

Cream the butter, add the grated almonds and then gradually the flour. Knead well and form into little rolls about i inch thick. Bend round into the shape of horns and bake on a buttered tin. While still hot, roll in castor sugar.

Mandelbrotchen
(Almond Cakes.)

10 oz. sweet almonds.	3 ground cloves.	A pinch of ground ginger.
3 eggs.	½ lb. flour.	
2 extra yolks.	4 oz. butter.	
4 oz. sugar.	A pinch of cinnamon.	

Cream the butter, add the sugar and the eggs and stir 30 minutes. Then add the spices, almonds and lastly the flour. Place in little heaps on a buttered tin and bake a golden brown.

Mandelringe
(Almond Rings.)

½ lb. sweet almonds.	15 bitter almonds.
6 oz. sugar.	4 yolks.
6 oz. flour.	1 teaspoonful ground cinnamon.
4 ground cloves.	½ teaspoonful ground ginger.

Beat the yolks and sugar 15 minutes to a froth and stir in the cinnamon, cloves and ginger and then the grated almonds and the flour. With this paste make little rings, brush them over with yolk of egg and poppyseeds (or chopped almonds, if preferred) and bake on a buttered tin in a moderate oven.

Zimmetstangen
(Cinnamon Sticks.)

4 whites of eggs.	¾ lb. sugar.
1 oz. cinnamon.	14 oz. pounded almonds.

Whisk the whites of eggs and stir with the sugar for 15 minutes. Then add the ground cinnamon and pounded almonds. Place little strips of this paste (about 3 inches long and ½ inch thick) on a buttered tin and bake in a moderate oven.

Glasuren
(*Icings.*)

Zitronen-Glasur
(Lemon Icing.)

½ lb. castor sugar.	4 tablespoonsful lemon juice.

Warm the lemon juice and sugar in a saucepan till lukewarm. Then spread at once over the cake to be iced. White wine, rosewater or fruit syrup may be substituted for the lemon juice.

Schokoladen-Glasur
(Chocolate Icing.)

4 oz. chocolate.	½ lb. sugar.	1 oz. sugar.
1 gill water	¼ oz. butter.	

Stir the sugar into the water and boil up in an enamelled saucepan. Then add the cocoa, chocolate and a very little butter, and boil till a slight skin begins to form. Then spread over the cake.

Spritzglasur

1 tablespoonful white wine *or* rose-water.	6 oz. castor sugar.
	½ teaspoonful lemon juice.

Mix all well together till a thick mass. Fill a firm, pointed paper bag, cut the tip of the bag off, fasten together at the top, and by pressing the thumb at that end, the icing is squirted out at the pointed end of the bag, so that patterns of all sorts can be traced at will on the surface of Torten and other cakes.

Punsch
(*Punch.*)

Eier-Punsch
(Egg Punch.)

2 eggs.	½ pint water.
2 extra yolks.	½ gill rum.
3 tablespoonsful lemon juice.	4 oz. sugar.
½ pint white wine.	

Beat to a froth the eggs, sugar, lemon juice and 1 gill cold water. Add the remainder of the water, boiling, and stir briskly till it comes to the boil. Then add the rum and serve the Punch at once.

Glühwein
(Negus.)

Bring to the boil, in a covered saucepan, 1 pint red wine, a piece of cinnamon, 2 cloves and 3 oz. sugar. Before serving, remove the cloves and cinnamon.

Weinschaum

Cider, Moselle or Rhine wine are suitable for this; the stronger the wine, the more sugar is necessary. On the average, reckon to 1½ pint wine, 7 oz. sugar, 4 whole eggs, 4 extra yolks and a little lemon peel. Put all into a saucepan and stir briskly till just on the boil. Then serve in glasses or cups.

Rotwein-Pansch
(Red Wine Punch.)

1½ pint light red wine.	1 pint Russian tea.	½ lb. sugar.
1 gill rum.	1 gill lemon juice.	

Bring all just to the boil and serve at once.

Himbeer-Punsch
(Raspberry Punch.)

1 pint red wine.	½ pint sweet raspberry syrup.
1 pint Russian tea.	1 gill rum.
1 gill lemon juice.	

Bring all just to the boil and if necessary sweeten with a little sugar. Other fruit syrups may be substituted for raspberry syrup, if desired.

Eis-Pansch
(Iced Punch.)

1 gill lemon juice.	1 lb. sugar.	4 whites of eggs.
¾ pint water.	1 gill orange juice.	
1 gill rum.	½ pint red wine.	

Boil up the sugar in the water and allow it to cool again. Then add the lemon and orange juice, wine and rum. Put into a freezing machine and, when half frozen, stir in the stiffly-whisked whites of eggs. Then allow to finish freezing and serve in wineglasses.

Bowle
(*Bowle.*)

The best combination for Bowie is half Rhine wine and half Moselle, only *real* Seltzer water being added. The chemically-prepared Seltzer water ruins the flavour of the wine.

It is important that the Bowie should not be too sweet and should be quite cold.

For Strawberry Bowie reckon ½ lb. wood strawberries to 2 bottles of wine. For Peach Bowie, the same quantity of peaches, which should be peeled, stoned and cut into several pieces. Sprinkle both strawberries and peaches respectively with ¼ lb. sugar, and pour over them ½ pint of wine. Stand in a cool place for ½ hour, well covered over. Then add the remaining wine. Ananasbowle (Pineapple Bowie) is prepared in the same way. Tinned pineapple or pineapple essence may be employed if the fresh fruit cannot be obtained.

Mai-Bowle

Pour a bottle of Moselle or cider on to a little bunch of .woodruff (Waldmeister) and stand on ice, closely covered over, for 30 minutes. Then melt 2 oz. sugar in ¼ pint water and mix with the wine, removing the woodruff and adding an orange, carefully peeled and cut into slices.

Kalte Ente

1 bottle good red wine.	¾ bottles real Seltzer water.
1 bottle light Rhine wine.	1 lb. ice broken up into small pieces.
1 gill lemon juice (strained).	7 oz. sugar boiled up in 1 gill water.

Mix all ingredients, except the Seltzer, and stand, closely covered over on ice, for at least 2 hours. Add the Seltzer just before serving.

Sellerie-Bowle
(Celery Bowle.)

Half a celery root.	4 oz. sugar.
1 bottle Moselle *or* cider.	½ gill rum.
½ gill water.	

Wash and peel the celery root. Cut into slices, sprinkle with sugar and pour the water and rum over. Stand, closely covered over, on ice. Then take out the celery and add the wine.

Bowie von Rot- und Apfelwein
(Red Wine and Cider Bowle.)

1 bottle red wine.	1 pint water.	1 orange.
4 oz. sugar.	1 bottle cider.	

Grate some of the rind of the orange on the sugar and boil up with half the water. Stand to get cool. Cut up the orange into slices (removing all the white and the pips) and pour the sweetened orange water on it. Leave on ice, covered over, for 30 minutes and then add the wine. Moselle may be substituted for the cider.

Bischof

1 bottle red wine.

3 oz. sugar.

½ teaspoonful bitter orange essence (Pomeranzen-Essenz) *or* a piece of Seville orange skin.

Pour a glass of wine over the essence, or skin and stand, covered over, for several hours on ice. Then add the remaining wine.

Kardinal

Prepare as the preceding recipe, but with white wine instead of red wine.

www.ingramcontent.com/pod-product-compliance
Lightning Source LLC
LaVergne TN
LVHW091255080426
835510LV00007B/267